The ESSENTIALS of

Business Management for Profit

Harvey C. Krentzman

And the Staff of Research and Education Association

Dr. M. Fogiel, Director

Research & Education Association
61 Ethel Road West
Piscataway, New Jersey 08854

THE ESSENTIALS®
OF BUSINESS MANAGEMENT FOR PROFIT

Printed in the United States of America

Library of Congress Catalog Card Number 99-70107

International Standard Book Number 0-87891-246-0

WHAT "THE ESSENTIALS" WILL DO FOR YOU

This book is a review and study guide. It is comprehensive and it is concise.

It is a handy reference source.

It condenses the vast amount of detail characteristic of the subject matter and summarizes the **essentials** of the field.

It will thus save hours of research and preparation time.

The book provides quick access to the important facts, principles, procedures, and management techniques in the field.

Materials needed for business management can be reviewed in summary form – eliminating the need to read and reread many pages of reference materials. The summaries will even tend to bring detail to mind that had been previously read or noted.

This "ESSENTIALS" book treats in an up-to-date, down-to-earth "shirt sleeves" fashion, production and marketing, purchasing and collections, financial management and management systems, accounting and taxation, and insurance and legal problems. Each chapter treats a topic in detail from varying viewpoints.

This book does not discuss theory for theory's sake. Its author's aim has been to achieve a practical balance between basic theory and day-to-day business practices in language which will allow the chief executive of a firm to translate the ideas presented into decisions and actions.

Dr. Max Fogiel
Program Director

CONTENTS

CHAPTER **PAGE**

Chapter 1

MARKETING, MERCHANDISING, ADVERTISING AND SALES PROMOTION

THE owner-manager of a small firm must recognize that, no matter how useful he feels his product or service to be, without a customer he has no business. Marketing is not restricted to the art of selling goods or services to the customer. The sale itself is the end result of a long series of marketing steps. These steps include the development of the product or service, pricing, distribution of the product, that is, the making of the service or product available, advertising, personal selling, promotion, and developing and directing the sales and/or service people. All these steps lead to the same goal for all businesses—the sale of a product or a service.

Marketing Tools

In a small firm, the responsibility for the sale lies with the owner-manager. Sudden increases and decreases in sales volume present an even greater burden to small businesses than to their large competitors who operate with large backlogs and large financial reserves. To overcome those advantages of his large competitors, the owner-manager of a small business must develop a marketing program which enables him to utilize to his best advantage the few marketing skills he has available. He does this by becoming familiar with the tools of marketing: merchandising, advertising and sales promotion.

Merchandising

People buy only when they want things or services more than money. Their desires may be easily understood as in the case of the basic necessities of life or they may be stimulated by outside suggestion, Merchandising, then reflects the efforts of the firm to "market the right merchandise or service at the right place, at the right time, in the right quantities and at the right price."

Merchandising is essentially a planning operation. It is the process of adjusting to customer demand the merchandise that is produced or offered for sale. It involves selecting and securing the appropriate products, ascertaining the proper quantities and quality to have in stock at the proper times and setting the appropriate prices for them.

Although the merchanidsing function is performed by manufacturers, wholesalers, retailers and service firms, it is a most critical function in retail and service operations. The service or retail firm has far less leeway in merchandising than do manufacturers and wholesalers. There is, for example, little opportunity in modern retailing to bargain with the customer over price. If the price, once set, is not to the consumer's liking, then the sale is lost. For manufacturers and wholesalers and some service firms on the other hand, much bargaining often takes place to arrive at the right price—a price that is mutually satisfactory to buyer and seller.

The owner-manager must maintain a clear understanding of the particular product or service need his firm is satisfying. He must create or adapt new product ideas that may be of value to the market he is serving. He must be alert to opportunities resulting from sudden changes in market needs. He must avoid the pitfalls created by the attitude of "we sold this product this way for the last 10 years and we will continue to sell it this way come rain or shine."

To be an effective merchandiser, the owner-manager must maintain a close watch on his market. He must continually ask the following questions about the needs his firm is satisfying:

WHO? Who are our customers, who are our competitors?

WHAT? What did the customer buy? What will he be buying? What is the potential market?

WHEN? When does he need our product or service? When will he buy our product or service?

WHERE? Where does he use our product? Where does he, or will, buy our type of product or service?

WHY? Why will he, or does he, buy our product or service?

HOW? How does he buy our product? In what quantity? How much will be pay?

The manager is responsible for relating these questions to the expected seasonal sales levels because rarely are sales evenly distributed throughout the year.

Advertising

Advertising is used primarily to *inform* the consumer of:

1. The availability of products or services.
2. The uses that buyers can make of them.
3. Besides informing, however, it must *convince* potential buyers that a particular product or service is superior to its competitors.

To inform and convince, the owner-manager of a small firm has the following advertising media: radio, television, newspapers, magazines, direct mail, handbills, billboards, and point-of-purchase aids. With very limited funds for advertising, he needs a good understanding of what advertising is likely to accomplish under different sets of marketing circumstances. Rather than spend the money available on a random unplanned basis, he is advised to establish a program. Frequently, because of a feeling of lack of availability of large sums of money for advertising, he just fritters these funds away instead of developing a practical program.

An important consideration in planning advertising in an established business is the firm's previous experience with outlays on advertising. A review of past advertising expenses and the direct and indirect benefits achieved is essential. As the owner-manager conceives his plan for using advertising to build profitable sales, he must consider the following: (1) whether he is selling a consumer or industrial product or a service; (2) the buying habits of his potential customers; (3) the character of his competition; (4) the price he can afford to sell at; (5) desired profit margins; (6) the scope of the market and (7) alternative methods of distribution.

The strategy used by an owner-manager in effectively using his advertising dollar calls for a concentrated, planned program. The buckshot approach with limited funds usually ends up with very poor results.

Dan Eisen [1] was operating a chain of three laundromats in the Midwest. He was frustrated at being unable to

[1] Names in all caselets and figures have been changed.

increase the level of sales in one of his stores. Every four to five months, he would advertise in the newspaper on a one-shot basis and at a very high expense. He ran a very clean and well-maintained operation and as a result had a very loyal clientele. But, Dan needed *more* customers, particularly for one of his units.

He happened to visit with the head of the marketing department at a nearby University and told him of his dilemma. The professor subsequently visited Dan's laundromats and asked questions. His analysis showed that Dan had no real advertising plan directed at the specific problem he wanted solved.

The professor and Dan developed a plan which included three successive mailings of handbills directed to potential customers in the immediate vicinity of the problem unit. The results of his mailings proved to Dan that his earlier advertising in newspapers was a waste of money. He had been directing his advertising to newspaper readers outside of his marketing areas.

By closely analyzing the problem to determine what kind of advertising, if any, is appropriate for a given marketing situation and spending the proper amount of time developing a hard-hitting advertising program, the owner-manager's chances of successfully using his limited funds are greatly improved.

Sales Promotion

Sales promotion consists of those activities which have the purpose of making other sales efforts (such as advertising) more effective. It may be directed toward the ultimate consumer, the trade, and salesmen. Sales promotion involves such things as creating special displays, offering premiums, running contests, distributing free samples, offering free introductory services, and demonstrating products. Frequently, sales promotions are coupled with special advertising programs.

Sales promotion is a widely used tool of the small business manager whether he is in retailing, distribution, or manufacturing. It may be used to promote the current product line or to sell slow-moving or obsolescent items in the inventory. An example of the latter in retail stores is the use of a "PM" or premium merchandise. The owner-manager can use "PM's" to turn over slow-moving items in order to have an "open to buy" position for new lines. Manufacturers offer retail salesmen "PM's" as a bonus to push their line over other competitive lines in the store.

Contests may be used as a sales promotion tool in motivating people to sell more. They are used by manufacturers, for example, to set up healthy competition among their salesmen.

The contest winner may be specified as the man with the highest percentage increase in sales over the prior years or the man who opens the most new accounts or the one who sells the highest number of units of a specific product. Contests may be more effective when the rewards include benefits for the wives of the salesmen. Frequent reporting of contest standings among the men is vital to maintain a sound competitive atmosphere. Reports of the standings of the men mailed to their wives during the contest usually develps more interest.

Contests may also be directed to the customer. Manufacturers can develop competition among their retail customers to achieve specific purchase volumes during a specified period of time. The rewards are usually in the form of added discounts, special field trips, or other prizes. Retailers frequently use contests to motivate their customers to buy higher ticket items or just spend more money in their store. The use of stamp plans by retailers, supermarkets, gas stations, and many others has been most successful in building increased sales volumes.

Special price deals can be used as a sales promotion tool. Deals are offered as a way to introduce new products as a "leader" to sell an entire line, or as an incentive to concentrate on a single buying source by means of a volume discount.

The owner-manager must control the use of sales promotion as a means of building sales. It is easy to be trapped into using a low profit sales deal as a continuous method of doing business. The net effect is then merely to cause a long-run reduction in price and gross profit. The manager must discipline himself and his organization when using sales promotions. It is sometimes wise to put the promotion in writing, spelling out all its elements including the closing or ending date.

Sales promotions can be very effective in improving the firm's sales performance, but, the manager must recognize the dangers as well as the opportunities which promotions bring.

Marketing and the Marketing Mix

Important changes in demand for particular products and services are continuously occurring. It is, therefore, a responsibility of the owner-manager to be responsive to such changes. As the firm grows, this responsibility increases. In order partially to meet it, the owner-manager must develop a concept of proper market timing. He must not lag behind the needs of the market. On the other hand, he must avoid the risks of moving appreciably ahead of what the market will accept. For these reasons, the marketing activity forces the manager to develop his skills and to experiment with various marketing approaches.

The manager's skill can be developed by recognizing the existence of the various elements in a "marketing mix." They include advertising, sales promotions, personal selling, trade shows, service activity, pricing and packaging. Because these elements in combinations produce sales, it is useful to think of them as composing a kind of "marketing mix." The owner-manager, as the marketing man, is a kind of "cook" who is continually experimenting with new blends and new kinds of ingredients. He hopes ultimately to come out with the ideal combination that will produce the highest amount of sales at the lowest practical cost. In a sense, he is balancing a number of variables in which the contribution of each element to the total result is often extremely difficult to measure.

The "market mix" for different types of products or services may vary widely. Even for the same class of product or service, competing companies may employ different combinations; changes in mix may well occur at different stages of the firm's growth and development. In the course of time, a company may change its marketing mix for a product as a result of changes in the many forces of the marketplace. The goal of the business in any instance is to find a mix at a given point of time that will prove to be profitable. To attain this end, the various elements have to be combined in a logically integrated program to conform to the market conditions bearing on the specific product or service.

Too frequently, the owner-manager of a small firm finds himself too busy running his current marketing program to review previous results. Unfortunately, he continues to make marketing decisions without the benefit of review and analysis of the effectiveness of the various elements of the mix. The unsuccessful firm is forced to look at its selling operations under the pressure of a crisis situation. The profitable growing firm doesn't need a review, or so the manager thinks. Why not review the various elements in the booming program? Is it possible that, in spite of success, some elements should be modified or changed to develop an even more effective marketing program?

A successful marketing mix requires developing the factual data regarding the firm's marketing costs. The owner-manager must establish some simple working rules with the firm's accountant and bookkeeper. The accumulation of accurate marketing expense information will require little extra office effort once the appropriate account classifications are established. Occasionally, problems may arise regarding the classification of an expense. As long as the bookkeeper posts the expenses in a consistent manner, the owner-manager can compare and analyze his costs effectively.

The manager will require a system that will highlight the results of the various "marketing mix" elements used by his firm. For example, the personal selling costs should be compared to the sales generated by each salesman. In situations where men are on straight commission, such an analysis is easily accomplished. Salesmen on salary will require a separate tally of their sales accomplishments. Where each of several salesmen contributes to a particular sale, a special set of rules is required. The situation is common in, for example, retail furniture stores, where one man starts the sale and another man closes it on another day.

Having the cost and performance data available will allow the manager to control his marketing program. The development of historical performance information for the various elements in the firm's "marketing mix" will enable him to use the limited marketing funds at his disposal effectively.

Development of the Marketing Mix

Guidelines for the owner-manager to follow as he endeavors to develop the ideal combination of marketing elements for the future are rarely available. Internally, he may look to the firm's historical pattern of spending and try to relate the performance of the various elements in the "marketing mix" to their cost. Externally, he may look to the programs used by his direct competitors. He may, for example, look to industry-wide statistics. But, in the final analysis, he must decide which elements will be used and how much money will be spent on each element.

Walter Cort manufactured a line of costume jewelry which he very successfully sold to retail jewelry stores. Throughout its first 5 years, Cort Jewelry Company located in a Midwestern city, used a marketing program containing the following elements:

ADVERTISING—Many ads were placed in the monthly trade magazines; Cort Jewelry spent nothing on advertising aimed directly at the ultimate consumer and, as a result, enjoyed no brand loyalty.

PROMOTIONS—Deals were offered in each month's advertising copy; by selling new items through such package deals, Walter succeeded in developing a large line of costume jewelry.

PERSONAL SELLING—There were no salesmen. Customers telephoning the company spoke to mere order-takers.

TRADE SHOWS—Walter Cort attended many regional and national trade shows in order to meet his customers in person.

SERVICE—Cort Jewelry was usually able to deliver merchandise faster than its competitors; also, the firm adhered to a liberal policy when it came to customer returns.

PRICING—Good quality items were offered at competitive prices; the Cort management used many pricing techniques designed to get the dealer to stock new items.

PACKAGING—There was some spending aimed at projecting an appealing image for the entire product line.

During its first five years, the Cort Jewelry Company had rapid growth. Walter Cort recognized that changes in the marketing mix might enable his firm to grow even faster. Pursuing this line of thought, Walter examined the firm's sales volumes for each area of the country over a three-year period. He found that the Southeast was seriously lagging behind the rest of the country.

Walter then decided to reduce somewhat his advertising outlays in Southeast region editions of the trade magazines. The money thus saved was used to hire a direct salesman for this region; Walter guaranteed this man a reasonable drawing account for 6 months, and offered to pay him anything extra which he could earn on a reasonable commission basis. To Walter's amazement, sales in the Southeast soon began growing rapidly —more rapidly than in any other part of the country. By resorting to personal selling methods, Cort Jewelry was able to merchandise its line in a manner that established higher gross profits for the firm. The salesman was able to concentrate his efforts on those jewelry stores that represented the largest growth potential for the company's line.

Cort Jewelry began to change its overall merchandising program as more salesmen were added. It began to develop different types of point of purchase displays and advertising mats for the retailer. These could now be used effectively since the salesmen were available to convince customers of their usefulness.

The change in the "market mix" caused Cort Jewelry to double its sales in two years and get a stronger foothold in the industry. Profits increased substantially. It wasn't too long before competitors put on a direct selling force, but Cort had a valuable head start. Walter Cort's willingness to innovate paid off. Many of Cort's other changes in marketing strategy were not as successful, but the firm's net position in the market was strengthened.

Many owner-managers of small firms fail to spend the necessary amount of time to review their marketing plans with an eye to creative improvement. Lack of courage, lack of know-how, and fear of change tend to keep the manager on a straight and narrow marketing program unless forced by competitive activities to innovate.

Determining Marketing Strengths and Weaknesses

The alert and interested owner-manager can overcome the obstacles to change if he has the desire to grow. He must, at all times, keep attuned to the changes in demand for his firm's product or service and adapt his firm's "marketing mix" so that the firm can maintain or improve its competitive position. He must consider which elements of the "marketing mix" are needed and how best to develop and execute an effective marketing program for the firm at that point in time. The owner-manager must relate the unique marketing needs of the firm to his personal capabilities and interests. He must endeavor to be as objective as possible and recognize the necessity of protecting his personal investment in the firm. Unfortunately, too frequently, entrepreneurs expose themselves to great personal financial risk by over-estimating their own marketing abilities.

As the manager evaluates the marketing needs of the firm, he must choose the exact "marketing mix" needed to develop profitable sales. He must establish *priorities* in the use of personal selling, advertising, sales promotions, packaging and pricing, within the limits established by the amount of sales needed and the funds available for the marketing program.

He must endeavor to treat the marketing needs of the firm objectively. At the outset, he should try to avoid developing a program around his personal activities, since they may be weak and insufficient to meet the sales objectives needed. He must candidly recognize the competitive marketing problem and how his firm's resources can best be employed.

In order for the manager to be able to evaluate or compare his knowledge and skills as a marketing man in a particular trade, it is important that he meet marketing people in the trade, so as to gain detailed industry information. If he desires to determine how his skills as a marketing man compare to those of others, he should become exposed to other selling people and marketing managers. This can be accomplished through friends and associates, trade suppliers and by joining marketing organizations. It might be possible to take certain occupational personnel tests as an additional means of determining how he compares to other salesmen. The need for objective self-appraisal is vital if the firm is to succeed.

Once the owner-manager determines his marketing capabilities and compares them to what appears to be the needs of the firm, he must determine which phases of the marketing program would be of greatest interest to him. The experience of Jim Dawson provides an example.

He owned and managed a drug jobbing firm in a Midwestern city. The particular line of drug items he distributed normally required a large amount of outside selling time to retail druggists. He realized, as he developed his firm's marketing program, that a number of salesmen would be needed. Although Jim was capable of doing the retail selling, he recognized that his efforts would be more effectively used by hiring and training men for the selling and servicing functions of his firm. He made himself available for the special needs of his men, and directed his own efforts and capabilities to the internal sales areas, to product development, to advertising and sales promotion, to pricing, and to packaging. This kept him very busy at the office. (This worked out especially well since Jim Dawson had no interest in traveling; he disliked staying away from home for weeks at a time.) It requires some degree of prudence for the owner-manager to determine how and where his personal marketing skills can best be used to strengthen the firm's selling activities. Jim understood his strengths and weaknesses in marketing, but was interested in improving his marketing skills. He knew the drug field in general from many years of experience as a salesman for another drug jobber.

To improve his marketing skills, Jim Dawson attended workshops and seminars given in his marketing area. These included local university evening adult education programs, trade courses developed by his trade association, and various marketing seminars presented by the local marketing, sales and advertising clubs. Over the years, Jim's marketing skills became sharpened. As his role from a "doer" to a "manager" developed, it was necessary for him to break his original job into many parts: sales administration, sales promotion, buying, order processing and customer service.

The owner-manager, as he evaluates the firm's marketing needs and personal capabilities and interests, must avoid the serious risks involved in over-estimating his personal strengths. As the firm grows, he is in a better position to compensate for his marketing voids or blind spots by hiring capable subordinates. Being in continuing contact with many suppliers, customers and service firms, he should always be on the lookout for the specialized staff he will need. By planning ahead in this way, he will be in a position to evaluate the potential of prospective employees over a period of time. He can arrange a number of interviews with the candidates thus reducing the chances of error in his selection.

The owner-manager must also develop an understanding of the importance of each key subordinate as he endeavors to grow and improve the profitability of his business. He must avoid the common weakness among owner-managers of comparing the performance of new members of his staff to himself, without giving the new employee a sufficient amount of time to develop the specific marketing experience needed in his particular industry. In many instances, the owner-manager half-consciously hopes that his newly hired subordinates will fail or be ineffectual. Actually, the boss needs to exert a high degree of self-discipline when he hires someone to attend to areas in which he personally is uninterested or weak. The owner must be sure to give the newly hired person a fair chance to perform; in fact, he should make a conscious effort to help each employee keep up to date and to grow in his job.

Balancing the Marketing Function

In order to ensure that his marketing program will be able to be effectively executed, the owner-manager needs a good understanding of the time demands that will be placed upon him by it. Such understanding will permit him to recognize in which phases of the firm's overall operations his time can best be utilized. The manager who plans ahead can exercise a greater degree of control over his personal time allocation than can the manager without a plan.

Periodically, the entrepreneur ought to re-evaluate the use of his time among the various marketing activities. He must carefully consider how much of his time to devote to advertising planning, to personal selling and to attending trade shows. It is common to find owner-managers spending a great amount of time doing personal selling—especially to customers of long standing. At the same time, there is a tendency to under-estimate the importance of these other marketing tools and strategies. Careful planning will make it feasible to delegate much or all of the personal selling to various subordinates. Of course, even after this has been done, the owner will continue to oversee the personal selling activity.

The function of marketing is to sell the firm's products or services in a manner that will yield the highest net profit in the long run. This requires: 1) keeping the firm operating at or near its peak capacity throughout the year; 2) selling at the highest prices that are acceptable in the long run; and 3) keeping marketing expenses pretty much on a par with those of competitors.

Outside Marketing Assistance

The growing small firm requires all the skills and talents available to their competitors. It cannot afford the luxury of a full-time marketing staff nor does it need such staff services at all times. Recognizing the part-time specialized skill needs in the small firm is the owner-manager's first step in taking positive action. The small firm may not need a full-time sales promotion manager, advertising manager, and product development manager, but it does need all their skills at intermittent points in time. It is the responsibility of the owner-manager to define these needs in the face of the imbalances or voids in his organization's marketing skills.

There exists a strong feeling among small business owners that an "outsider" can be of little or no value to a business. The outsider is often accused of:

1. Lack of knowledge of the industry and of the firm's product line, or
2. An inability to understand the people working in this particular company.

Opposition to the use of outsiders also arises from fear of wasting time and money. There's a general feeling that the owner-manager and his staff can do things better irrespective of the marketing skills involved.

Managers must be able to separate the technical skill needs from the managerial skill needs. Outside idea sources can be of real value in creating and suggesting new ideas and approaches which are of general marketing value. By blending the general information presented by the outside source with the specific marketing and product knowledge of the owner-manager, very useful results can be attained. As a relationship progresses, the outsider's knowledge of the technical elements of the small firm increases. As the gap in technical understanding becomes less and less, his opportunities to be even more helpful are magnified.

Outside sources that may aid the entrepreneur could include the following:

1. Advertising agencies.
2. Customers.
3. Direct mail firms.
4. General marketing consultants.
5. Market researchers.
6. Packaging specialists.
7. Product development consultants.
8. Sales promotion consultants.
9. Salesman employment agencies.
10. Site selection specialists.
11. Suppliers.
12. Traffic and warehousing consultants.
13. Various local, State and Federal agencies.

The relationship between the outside source and the firm may be in some cases on a no-fee service basis such as those of suppliers or government agencies. In other instances, the services of outside sources may be obtained on a fee basis. The fee arrangement may be on a per diem, retainer, per project or contingency basis.

Once an outside marketing advisor has been selected, the owner-manager must then relate the specific marketing facts to him.

For example, Mel Fine who owns a beauty parlor was considering the advisability of expanding his operations to many units. All of his financial and economic questions could be satisfactorily answered by his accountant, but Mel sorely needed advice regarding the feasibility and cost of a marketing plan for a multi-unit beauty parlor operation. After some looking around the community for an advertising man who had had experience in small multi-unit retail store operations, Mel met Herb Williams who headed an advertising agency. After an initial interview, Mel felt that Herb's background and experience were in line with what he had in mind.

Mel retained Herb Williams to give him the marketing backup he needed. Mel invested a grat deal of time at the outset giving his advertising man all the facts on current and planned operations. Herb Williams asked Mr. Fine many questions on problems that had gone unrecognized. Mr. Williams took the information back to his office. After a few weeks of research, he returned with many new ideas and suggestions. Both men worked out a modified plan for expansion which included the expected costs and results.

Although Mel had invested time and risked some funds in retaining the Williams Advertising Agency, he had obtained a more realistic picture of his project and could make a more accurate decision. It turned out that Mr. Fine went ahead with his expansion plan. He retained Mr. Williams and worked with him on all marketing matters that developed. He, in effect, had a skilled part-time advertising manager on his team.

The major resistance among owner-managers of small firms to employing part-time outside assistants is their cost. Frequently, little thought is given to the possible results. In order to avoid the cost fears, the entrepreneur should screen his outside sources before employment. He should check into their credentials and perhaps talk with some of the other firms with whom they are or have been associated. Given the varying needs of different-sized firms, the manager should note the experience of the outsider in firms of the same size as his own. (The marketing requirements of small firms are, in general, quite different from those of larger firms). Usually, the outsider will not only have to advise and suggest, but will also help carry out the programs decided on.

Summary

In the fast-moving competitive market place, the businessman competes with well-trained and well-organized competitors. Survival depends upon his ability to find market opportunities and capitalize on them quickly and effectively. Thus he must at all times be alert to changes in the market his firm is serving; he must innovate and stay ahead of his competition.

To be successful, the owner-manager must become an effective merchandiser of the product or service of his firm. He must also learn how to use the essential marketing tools of advertising, sales promotion, pricing, packaging, etc. Using these tools will help him to most effectively utilize his limited marketing funds and to organize more effectively those marketing management skills that may be available in his firm. Simply stated, if the manager does not understand the marketing tools available, he can only be less effective than any competitor who possesses a better grasp.

Understanding and using the "marketing mix" concept will allow the owner-manager to analyze his firm's past and present marketing costs and marketing results as a basis for planning future programs. The importance of setting up accounting categories for marketing expenses and developing a method or system for accumulating marketing results cannot be overstated.

The owner-manager should evaluate his personal competency as a marketing manager. Awareness of his marketing weaknesses and areas of disinterest will help him to compensate for them when he staffs his organization. He must be wary of his own ego when he hires marketing people to supplement his own lack of skills. Above all, he must maintain his objectivity if he hopes to reach the sales and profit objectives he sets for his firm.

Many highly skilled outside resources in the technical and managerial aspects of the marketing program are available on a part-time basis. The manager who is familiar with the availability of those outside services from his trade and local community can call upon them as they are required. He then has available, at relatively low cost, the necessary marketing staff assistance to help him compete more effectively.

The overall effectiveness of the marketing program depends upon the owner-manager's ability to balance his time between marketing, operations, finance and people. In marketing, he must avoid concentrating on personal selling to the neglect of other marketing tools. He must always try to sell his product or service at the highest possible prices and at the same time keep marketing expenses level with those of his competitors. His chances of achieving these objectives are improved if he has a marketing plan that will best use his limited marketing funds.

Chapter 2

PRODUCTION

THE alert, aggressive owner-manager can uncover many growth opportunities for his small manufacturing enterprise. If he understands the market for his product, he will be freer to focus his attention on the shop. Regardless of his firm's size, he must continue to develop and improve the shop's flexibility, creativity, and productivity.

To keep operating competitively, the owner-manager must know the tools of production management and how to use them. He should keep up to date on product planning, plant layout, production methods, and quality control. And he should learn the proper conditions for installing production standards, incentive plans, job evaluation, and other types of production controls.

The Tools of Production Management

A manufacturing firm is an organization of men, materials, and machinery whose primary objective is to produce goods for profit. The responsibility of the owner-manager in the small firm requires him to develop his production management skills to the utmost.

Types of Production

Manufactured products may be classified as either consumer or industrial, and they may be produced on a standard basis, a job-lot or batch basis, or a process basis. Products ready for consumption are called consumer goods; those which will be used for further manufacturing are called industrial goods. Modern mass production (or standardized production) uses highly repetitive operations to produce large quantities of standard items. When customers demand variety or want products made to particular specifications, the job-lot or batch method of production is used. Some custom manufacturers produce only "one of a kind"; others may manufacture a substantial volume of similar products, but fewer than the number produced by mass production systems. When a product can be produced only by a controlled sequence of operations, process production is used. Once the process is begun, it must be continuous for physical and economic reasons. Examples are the production of fruit preserves, juice drinks, bakery products, and the like.

The Small Manufacturer's Advantage. The unique capabilities found among small manufacturing firms stem from the creativity, flexibility, and productivity generated by their owner-managers, who are in direct contact with their production foremen and operators. The presence of the owner-manager very often motivates the organization to move quickly and inspires the work force to strive for high levels of productivity.

Both custom and job-lot production present a number of difficulties to the larger manufacturer. Job-lot production uses general-purpose equipment, able to do many tasks, and it requires a flexible organization. Custom manufacturing requires a highly skilled work force. Because the sequence of operations on each product is usually different, production engineering and supervision are difficult tasks, and coordination of the various operations is a challenging problem. Operating costs, as well as cost per production unit, will usually be much higher than in mass-production processes. The buyer of custom products is usually willing to pay a higher price for them. Because nonstandard custom products make unusual demands on a manufacturer, chances are the small firm can satisfy these needs better than can the larger competitor, whose setup is organized for mass production.

Jack Daley, who owns Specialized Motors, Inc., started as a small machine shop operator. Needing a special type of one-half horsepower motor, he searched for days before finding a small firm that designed and manufactured small and medium-size specialized motors. This

firm quoted him a 3-month delivery, but the large standard horsepower motor manufacturers quoted even longer delays and seemed very little interested in taking an order from him.

After further research, Jack decided that small motor manufacturing could be a good field to get into. He found an engineer with design and production knowhow and began to turn out custom designed motors—expecting to limit his service, initially, to his local marketing area. Within 2 years, however, business had increased so much that he had hired a hundred people. Even with the larger production, Jack has made a point of keeping close control over the operation of the business to insure that his customers get a quality product delivered as promised and at a fair price. Specialized Motors, Inc., is a good example of the way a small manufacturer can be of real service. Because of the limited size of the market and the difficulties involved in designing and producing his specialized product in small quantities, Jack's skills in direct management will go far to assure his firm's success.

Other Opportunities. In addition to the opportunities for growth and profitability in short run job-lot manufacturing, there are a number of others, such as in fields:

Requiring a unique capability to produce or process a narrow line of products.

Based on seasonal cycles, with low capitol investment, where style changes create need for short production cycles (for instance, clothing, jewelry, shoes).

Requiring fast service (such as printing, photoengraving, specialty chemicals).

Where small firms function as converters of new chemical products developed by large firms (such as aerosol packaging, plastic injection, vacuum and blow molding, extrusion, printing and conversion of polyethylene).

Whose industries have low volume requirements.

Where bulky or heavy products demand local manufacturing facilities and fast service (such as the production of barrels, upholstery, and mattresses).

When To Avoid Competition

The small manufacturer must avoid competing with large mass production firms—especially when:

Major capital equipment is required (such as in steel, autos, tires and tubes).

National and international distribution organization is needed (as in the case of most large volume industrial and consumer products).

Extension of large credit lines is vital for effective sales distribution.

Extensive in-house technical capacity for research and development is necessary to develop new basic materials and products.

The owner-manager must determine the particular need his firm will be able to serve competitively, recognizing the above factors. His advantage relates to his ability to produce short run goods cheaper than his larger competitors. As his markets grow and consolidate, he must carefully watch the effects on his particular productline. Markets are rarely static; changes in markets and technology occur all the time.

The owner-manager should also recognize the many opportunities open as subcontractors or suppliers of larger manufacturing, distribution, or retailing organizations. Frequently the order of one large retailing firm for a specific product can be the base from which a very successful small manufacturing enterprise can be built.

Herb Anderson, having spent more than 10 years selling women's shoes to large retail chain organizations, developed some very good relations with a number of buyers. Deciding to go into business for himself, Herb formed the Anderson Shoe Corp. and leased a plant. As customers, he acquired three major chains, which consume about 50 percent of his production, and several smaller independent retailers and shoe wholesalers. His strategy of using a few large firms as the basis for his business is very common among small firms. But he showed good judgment in developing a broad base of smaller independent customers.

Product Planning

An owner-manager's success is often related to his ability to develop effective product strategy. To win customer orders, his products must be distinguishable from those of his competitors. At the same time, they must be profitable to make and sell. With good planning, an owner-manager can develop products that will most fully use his firm's particular variety of skills and abilities and its fixed stock of machinery and equipment. A particular product may require the use of skills that can be hired; but purchased operations should be kept to a minimum. In planning his product, the owner-manager should make every possible use of his firm's in-house skills.

Many unique design, service, and quality advantages can be added to his product because of his closeness to production. And such special additions should bring enough higher price or increased volume of business to justify the added production costs.

Plant Layout

Plant layout—the determination of the particular relationship between equipment and operations which will result in the greatest degree of economy and effectiveness—is very important in achieving lowcost, efficient production. Purposes of developing a good layout are as follows:

To keep material and supply-handling costs to a minimum.

To make sensible use of floor space—receiving space, shipping area, elevators, etc.

To make effective use of machinery and equipment.

To make best use of employees' time.

To control overall production.

To keep effective control of inventories and work process.

To stay flexible to allow for expansion and consolidation.

Rapid changes in the small manufacturing firm make it imperative that the owner-manager develop a strategy to handle product changes and rapid increases and decreases in demand.

Many sudden increases in demand can be met by working overtime. If demand still exceeds output, a second shift (either partial or full) can be added. Sometimes, a combination is necessary: some employees will work half time on the day shift and half time on the night shift. This arrangement also helps solve the problem of spreading out the regular supervisory people.

When demand continues and expansion of space is necessary, the owner-manager must avoid getting a chopped-up plant layout. In developing the original plant layout, the owner-manager should try to locate heavy machinery where additional heavy equipment can be easily added later. Inventories, offices, etc., can be more easily moved into new quarters than can heavy equipment. Not only will this system save costs and time in moving heavy equipment, it will also avoid wasting large investments in leasehold improvements. This conservative approach makes sense when the period of increased demand for a product is unknown. The most efficient plant layout for the small manufacturer is of little value without the necessary volume of available work at profitable prices.

The owner-manager must also be careful in considering new plant construction or long-term lease obligations for greatly expanded production space. Frequently, it is possible to sublet space under satisfactory termination conditions and reduce the risks involved in becoming obligated for greatly expanded space.

The owner-manager should understand the mechanics of laying out a plant. Each basic type of production has particular layout needs. Plant layout depends primarily on the type of production processes used. Volume of production to be attained governs ultimate space requirements. Final layout should express the purpose of the plant and must be built around the process.

For locating machinery, the two general types of layouts used are based on the process used and the product made. In the process type layout, all machines or operations for a specific function are grouped together in one department, and the product travels from department to department. This arrangement maintains a high degree of production flexibility. It is used when a product is not standardized, when the volume of each job-lot is low, and when many types of products are being made.

The product type layout is used for straight-line production. All the pieces of production equipment needed to produce a single product are grouped together, and the material flows directly from one operation to another. This arrangement, less common in the small firm than the process type layout, requires large-scale production of a standarized product. It keeps work-in-process to a minimum, reduces delays in production, and requires less floor space.

As the owner-manager reviews the growth and reduction of the various products in his line, he may find that he can use a combination of the process and product type plant layouts. He should periodically analyze his product line and diagram on paper the production processes used in his plant. Then he will be able to take maximum advantage of his space and maintain a high level of plant production.

Production Methods

After reviewing his plant layout, the next step is to review the production methods and standards used. When the owner-manager is able to stay in the shop, he can observe methods and production rates; but when he begins to rely on others, he must develop some way to know what is going on in the shop.

The essential aim of methods improvement is to eliminate the waste of time, materials, and machinery that occurs in most jobs. It is not intended that production be increased through harder work by the operator, but that through better tooling or ways of doing the job the operator will be able to produce more with less effort.

The owner-manager should see to it that all repetitive jobs be subjected to a methods study. The typical approach to methods improvement is comprised of the following:

1. Select the job.
2. Break down the job into its elements.
3. Question the job.
4. Develop a new method.
5. Install the new method.

Although the owner-manager lacks time to study methods improvement, he can direct his foreman and key subordinates to take action. He can also help create a favorable climate among his employees for developing new and better practical methods of doing their jobs.

Once the owner installs a job method which is accepted by the operator, then some production goals must be established. Production standards, when scientifically developed, are a valuable tool for the manager; he can use them in devising a wage incentive program, knowing and controlling labor costs, measuring the effectiveness of supervision, and helping to plan production.

Frequently, arguments occur between worker and foreman (or foreman and owner) concerning the production expected from a given operator. With production standards, everyone will know what is expected. Of course, when operators are always changing and when only short runs are being made, it is impractical to establish exact production standards. Then, the operation that is performed, or that is being estimated so that a price can be quoted, should be compared to the most similar operation in the shop, and the rate of output predicted accordingly.

Inspection and Quality Control

The owner-manager must determine the level of quality he expects for his firm's product or service. Quality can be defined in terms of desired characteristics such as dimension, strength, shape, finish, color, and workmanship. For a particular item, quality would be measured by the particular standards set, and any deviation from these standards would be a variation in quality. However, inspection and quality control activities do not by themselves make acceptable products. Acceptable products are made by machine operators and production supervisors. A supervisor is responsible for producing and measuring quality; he must be quality conscious. He must make his men quality conscious by instilling in them the desire to produce and maintain quality.

Types of Inspection. As a firm grows and it becomes more difficult to produce and measure quality, a separate inspection department will be needed. Types of inspection include:

1. Remedial and preventive.
2. Centralized and floor.
3. Raw materials, work in process, and finished products (or final).
4. Visual.
5. Nonvisual.

Remedial inspection catches defects that have already occurred. Preventive inspection concentrates on maintaining the accuracy of manufacturing processes in order to avoid defects and waste. Centralized inspection gathers items in a separate place set aside for it. Floor inspection takes place at the point of production. Raw materials inspection occurs as soon as supplies are received, or before they are used. Work-in-process inspection may be in the form of floor inspection or centralized inspection. Finished products inspection is the final check made before shipment. Visual inspection uses color, contour, roughness, or any other characteristic that can be checked by sight. Nonvisual inspection involve chemical analyses, tests of tensile strengths, etc.

To take fullest advantage of product planning, plant layout, production methods, and inspection processes, the owner-manager (or his key subordinates) must be experienced or trained in the technical aspects of the product and the production process. This technical knowhow may come from the experience within the firm, from suppliers, trade associations, technical engineering consultants, or from many other sources.

Various Tools of Production Management

In addition to technical management tools, there are other less technical devices used to manage the plant. These tools relate to the designing and manufacture of products to the quality and quantity levels desired.

Production Standards

Production standards are a valuable tool in setting incentive wages, costing the operation, and planning production. Time standards are valuable after the proper production method has been established. The three methods most used to establish accurate and fair production standards are: (1) time study, (2) standard time data, and (3) predetermined time values.

Time study is the oldest and most widely used method among small firms. Its success largely depend upon the ability and experience of the man making the study. The only equipment needed is a stopwatch and a time study form; the steps involved are:

1. Record the operation data.
2. Break down the job into its elements.
3. Observe the job; record the time.
4. Analyze the time study.
5. Compute the production standard for the operation.

After a number of time studies have been made of related jobs, a pattern should develop in the allowed time for each of the various elements. For any group of related studies, a comparison sheet can be drawn up; and if enough studies are available, elemental time standards can be developed for each constant factor. From such information, called standard time data, it is possible to determine the production standard for other related but untimed jobs without resorting to another time study.

Systems of predetermined time values have also been developed—including: Methods-Time Measurement (MTM), Work Factor, the Segar-System, and Basic Motion-Time Standards. No matter how well these systems are developed, their use will not eliminate the need for stopwatch time study.

Because of closeness to operations, the owner-manager of a small manufacturing firm usually doesn't find it necessary to set written time standards. He can directly communicate the production levels expected, and he is around to check on his employees' daily production. As his firm expands and he spends less time in the shop, he will usually need more formal production standards.

Wage Incentive Plans

Wage incentives are a powerful production tool. Rewards can go to those employees whose productivity, skill, effort, and attitudes are commendable. The owner-manager must, however, recognize the potential danger of rewarding employees as a result of unwritten and informal evaluations. As his firm grows, he will need to set up a more formal wage incentive plan.

Formal plans will most likely relate to the direct production force while informal incentive plans will cover foremen, executives, and indirect labor groups. The incentive plan should be simple and easy to administer. It must be clearly understood and accepted by the work force if it is to achieve its purposes of increased production, reduced waste, and better use of machinery.

The basic kinds of incentive plans are:

1. Straight piecework.
2. 100 percent premium.
3. Split premium.
4. Task and bonus.

The oldest and most widely used is piecework. The other systems have been devised to overcome some of the disadvantages of piecework, such as complete dependence on the time study. Straight piecework is perhaps the easiest to develop, install, and maintain; for that reason, it is most often found in small plants.

The Job Evaluation Program

The work force in a small firm must be very flexible so as to service the customers' sudden requirements. Often, an employee must do several jobs even though he is skilled in only one or two operations. But as a firm, and its work force grows, full-time specialists in each trade can be developed. At this point, a job evaluation program should be considered.

The job evaluation process determines the relative value of jobs in an organization. It reviews the jobs performed, not the persons performing them. It is not concerned with the personality, ability or character of a man doing a job. The job evaluation process seeks to establish a clearly understood difference between jobs—using work performed as the basis for distinction. Job evaluation is not an exact measuring tool, but an orderly approach calling upon management judgement.

Job evaluation is a useful tool for the owner-manager of a small firm. Chances are he employs a number of men doing the same (or similar) work. Each feels he deserves wages as high as those of the other. The manager must setup and maintain fair wage rates. A satisfactory job evaluation program will establish a fair and equitable wage structure related to jobs rather than to men. In very small shops it will, of necessity, include jobs with a very broad description covering many functions. As the firm grows, job evaluations will tend to become more specialized more specific.

The Merit Rating System. Once a job evaluation program is established, a merit rating system will help establish fair wage rates for employees. Merit rating evaluates each employee's performance and progress and rewards him for above-average performance. The rating is a systematic and impersonal method for determining the relative measure of each individual. It is sometimes called performance rating. Essentially then, job evaluation determines the rate range for a job, and merit rating sets the wage within the range for each man doing the job.

Merit rating is based upon the following commonly used factors:

1. Quality and quantity of work performed.
2. Cooperativeness.
3. Initiative.
4. Dependability.
5. Attendance.
6. Job knowledge.
7. Ability to work with others.
8. Safety and personal habits.

Each factor can be evaluated as: superior, above average, average, below average, or poor. Or a point system can be used: superior (40), above average (35), average (30), below average (25), and poor (20).

Job evaluations and merit ratings can help the owner-manager be objective in his pay scales for both long time key subordinates and other employees. Usually, the close relationship between the owner-manager and his employees creates a tendency to give raises when times are good and to keep wages stable during slack periods. The effective use of these tools should lead to a more fair and equitable wage payment program.

Production Control

The owner-manager of a small manufacturing firm must understand production control and how it relates to serving his customers better and to gaining greater profits for his firm. It provides an overall plan to coordinate men, materials, and machinery. This calls for the control of production times, processes, and methods of work; these include the scheduling and routing of work through the shop. A poor plan leads to additional cost, loss of output, confusion, and perhaps a poor product.

Production controls can help insure continuity of effective production. They can detect variations from the production plan and then specify the necessary corrective action. Inspection systems, paper systems, and operating procedures are essential parts of the control mechanism. Men and machines must be kept busy at all times if the firm is to succeed. This requires a steady flow of raw materials, good coordination among departments, and adequate preparation for emergencies, rush orders, and development of samples or prototypes.

A five-man shop, to be effective, requires little more than a few written schedules and the manager's memory. But, as a firm grows, the boss must give more time to other phases of the business, and problems in production planning and control may develop. Frequently, production planning and controls are the first "overhead" jobs established in a growing firm.

Cost Control

Cost control—particularly for pricing and, therefore, for volume—is vital in the struggle to achieve higher profit. Too frequently, the small firm depends entirely on annual or semi-annual profit-and-loss statements for cost control. This is not effective control. The profit-and-loss statement shows the profits of the company for a particular period, but it fails to explain *why* profits were as shown, and *where* costs were out of line. Every small firm must have a cost control program to provide some of the data needed to run the firm properly. For example, certain operating ratios can be developed from the profit-and-loss statement. If 40 percent of every revenue dollar is spent on direct labor, as in a machine shop, that would be the vital area for control. On the other hand, when materials are the greatest cost, as they are in a chemical plant, they are the cost element needing the closest control. The clothing manufacturer, having approximately equal costs for labor and materials would have to decide which one to concentrate on.

By focusing first on the main element of cost, the owner will be using his time and effort most effectively. Later, he can turn his attention to other kinds of costs—in proportion to the amount of money he spends on each and the opportunities he has for reducing them.

The Cost Gathering System. Once he understands the broad picture of operational costs, the manager must learn as much as possible about the costs of specific products. To do this, he will need a system for collecting actual cost data. It need not be elaborate, complicated, or expensive. Money invested in the development and maintenance of cost controls will be recovered when the system sends out a warning of danger. Such a system can also be very useful in checking original cost estimates with actual performance figures.

A cost-gathering system is unnecessary in many small firms because the owner-manager spends sufficient time in the shop to know the rate of production of each employee. To accumulate labor applied to each job and check out nonproductive time against the weekly direct labor payroll would be too cumbersome and impractical. And in many shops, the number of jobs and the speed with which they are done would make a complete cost control program unwise.

Cost Estimates. The owner-manager must know what his costs are. He must know how much to charge for a given product or service. He should have some measure of how much a given job did cost compared with how much he had expected it to cost. He should know how the volume produced in the shop will affect his profits. And he should have some guidelines for circumstances that would cause him to decline to bid for a very competitive job.

To control costs, many small business firms successfully use a written estimate of cost for each job of any consequence. (See figure 1. The example given is a garment manufacturer; it could be any of numerous other types of firms; the principles are the same.) Once the job estimated becomes an order, the factors used in the estimate become the labor and materials standards that the shop should strive to surpass. These estimates are issued to the shop with the production order (figure 2)—giving the shop foreman and operators a goal to strive for. Frequently, each department will note on a separate cost sheet the time actually spent on the job.

The shop foreman can set up a simple schedule noting the estimated time (as given in the production order) by which the job should be finished. Then daily, he can check on the operator's performance and tell at a glance how the job is progressing. This type of supervision by key subordinates and occasional spot checking of jobs by the owner-manager (preferably while the job is in prcess) tend to keep a certain amount of pressure in the shop and helps realize the *manager's* production expectations. Depending on what his checking reveals, the owner can take steps to reduce the cost of production or accept the rate of production for a given operation and use it more effectively on cost estimates of future jobs.

The cost of materials requires the serious attention of the owner all the way from checking multiple sources of supply to supervising incoming freight, receiving, stocking, production shrinkage, and storage of finished goods.

As part of his overall program of cost control, the owner-manager *must* keep a close watch on production materials used in his firm. Material costs must always be closely figured in making cost estimates of prospective jobs; and materials left over from previous jobs may cause the owner-manager to accept a very competitive order so as to be able to work off old inventory.

The Formal Cost System. As a firm grows, a more formal cost system is necessary. Designed to suit the needs of basic types of production techniques, the commonly used cost sytems are: (1) job cost, (2) process cost, and (3) standard cost.

In the job cost system, the cost elements for each order being worked on in the plant are collected separately. The system is most used in small firms producing special products to customers' specifications—such as machine shops, construction companies, etc.

Figure 1—Cost Estimating Form for Garments

STYLE & COST SHEET

Style No. ____________ **Date** ____________

MATERIALS:

Goods—Yds. ________ Cost Per Yd. ________	________
Sponging	________
Lining	________
Zip. ________ Butt. ________ Trim. ________	________
Belt	________
Pleating	________
TOTAL MATERIAL COST	________

LABOR:

Cutting	________
Outside Contractor	________
TOTAL LABOR COST	________

TOTAL GARMENT COST = Direct Labor + Direct Materials ________

Selling Price (Established by Market) ________

Gross Profit (Selling Price—Garment Cost)

MATERIAL **DESCRIPTION**

Type ____________

Mill ____________

Patt. # ____________

The continuous process cost system is used where processing of each product goes through the same operations—such as bottling, the food processing plants, gasoline refineries, and chemical plants.

The standard cost system uses predetermined cost standards derived from past experience and industrial engineering studies. It compares actual costs with the standards, and variation is reviewed for cause. The standard is intended to represent what cost *should be*, under specified set of conditions, and must be revised whenever methods, prices, or other related factors change.

Using Production Tools in Expansion

In too many small firms, the owner-manager bases his decisions on intuition, speculation, or incorrect data—though accurate and useful information would be available if the right production tool were employed. Often, profits are lost because available production tools are unknown, or if known are not used for fear of expected additional cost. To get best results, the owner-manager must know the right time to introduce production standards, incentive plans, production scheduling, job evaluations, merit ratings, cost controls, and the other tools available.

The owner-manager is so close to his operation that frequently he becomes conditioned to his routine. He knows intimately almost every facet of his business; but when his firm grows, there is so much to keep track of that he begins to miss details. New employees produce less and make errors. Customers begin to complain about delivery. New production systems are needed, along with the necessary staff trained to put them into effect. The owner-manager faces a serious challenge. Somewhere along the line, he should have added key subordinates and trained them to assume some of the responsibilities of managing the firm. And he must understand that when he does, he will have higher overhead costs until the results of the production system begin to pay off.

Charley D'Mare owned and operated a successful wholesale hardware distribution firm. In 4 years his sales volume grew about 25 percent each year. But Charley began having a very serious problem in his office and warehouse. The firm was unable to get orders processed, packed, and shipped in 1 to 2 days (which it had always done, heretofore). Deliveries were taking up to a week even though Charley had beefed up his office and warehouse staff.

He had added two girls to the two already working on order processing, but orders were still late in getting out to the warehouse. He had added three men to the six already working in the warehouse, but the number of shipments each day increased only slightly. Charley pushed his office and warehouse groups, but this only caused confusion and dissension among the old and new employees. The speed of servicing customers' orders was increased, but the effectiveness of the newer people remained low.

D'Mare Hardware called in a group of consultants, who quickly set up some new systems and procedures. They date-stamped every order received; set up a program for measuring the order typists' daily work; and

Figure 2—Production Order Form for Job-Lot Shop

PRODUCTION ORDER **00151**

CUSTOMER ORDER NO.	WHEN TO SHIP	SALES REP.	PROMISE	DATE

SOLD TO	SHIP TO

TERMS	CONTRACT NO.	INSPECTION		SHIP VIA
		YES	**NO**	

QUANTITY ORDERED	DESCRIPTION

WINDING		ASSEMBLY	FINISHING	ENGINEERING		INVENTORY		PRODUCTION MGR.	
MACHINE	EST. HRS.	ESTIMATED HOURS	ESTIMATED HOURS	SIGNATURE	DATE	SIGNATURE	DATE	SIGNATURE	DATE

MATERIAL REQUIRED	UNIT	TOT. REQ.	AVAIL.	ORD. QUAN.	DATE ORD.	P. O. NUMBER	VENDOR	DATE DUE	FOLLOW UP

SCREEN

DATE	QUAN. SHIPPED	PACK SLIP TO	BALANCE	DATE	QUAN. SHIPPED	PACK SLIP TO	BALANCE

determined the number of orders and items that could be expected each hour from the experienced girls. The consultants counted the number of orders received daily on the phone and by mail. They figured the production required from an experienced typist and set up a program to train each of the girls to achieve the standard. And as a production incentive, they introduced a merit-rating system based on number of orders typed. Within a short time, three girls could handle the flow of orders which had grown even larger, and the least outstanding typist was transferred to the bookkeeping area.

The consultants studied the warehouse layout and order-picking routines. They found from descriptions of work activities that all of the warehousemen received goods, put them in stock, picked orders, packed them, and did the necessary paper work. The result was a great waste of effort and skill.

The consultant set up a new job pattern, establishing specific primary jobs for each man, and allowing him to switch to other jobs only in emergencies. Each of the new jobs was evaluated, and the man best skilled for it was assigned to it. The newer, less skilled men were given the less skilled jobs, and were expected to improve their skills (and promotion possibilities) over a certain period of time. As in the office, production procedures were established, and fair production standards were set. For example, each picker of small hardware items was expected to pick three average orders of 10 items each, or 30 items, every hour. The receiver was expected to receive and put into stock about 40 items per day.

Within 2 months, two of the three men recently added were found to be unnecessary. D'Mare Hardware was back in balance, delivering within 2 days of receipt of an order; and Charley D'Mare could spend more of his time building up the firm's sales in a very competitive industry.

The consultants made effective use in the office and the warehouse of tools commonly thought of as being useful only in the shop. They paid close attention to warehouse layout, work flow, and production methods; then they put into effect such tools as produtcion standards, incentive plans, production control, job descriptions and evaluations, merit ratings, and cost controls.

These tools could also be used in many retail and service firms. For example, if a retail firm has trouble in its credit and collection department, a study could be made of the number of credit applications received daily, and these could be graded according to certain standards. The time required to clear the various types of credit risks could be figured, and the cost of performing this credit operation could be determined. Once significant factors were measured, new approaches should be considered, and the changes indicated should be made in method, in work standards, and in employee motivation.

As a firm grows, many functions which were minor become more important. If the owner-manager fails to develop a more formal approach to the systems and procedures involved, and if he also fails to develop the necessary staff, he may find himself buried in a pile of details. He will probably even be performing those details ineffectively and will be wasting much of his efforts because he doesn't have the time he needs to straighten them out.

The owner-manager need not establish rigid, formally written programs. But, he must avoid outmoded methods and must continuously update the firm's productivity.

Systems, Procedures, and Paperwork—Importance

As a firm grows, the owner-manager must keep track of an increasing volume of business activities, ranging from the receiving of merchandise to the promising of deliveries. At some point or other in this expansion, he can become enmeshed in overwhelming detail. He will be approached by his customers, suppliers, and employees concerning numerous routine and nonroutine problems; and if he hasn't laid plans beforehand, his memory will falter and errors will crop up. For example, the bookkeeper may have been instructed to get the boss's approval on invoices before making payment. But before the boss can approve an invoice, he will have to check with his warehouse employees to verify the quantity of goods received. The result can be lost discounts as well as wasted time for the bookkeeper. Also, the warehouse people who plan deliveries of merchandise will be held up on shipments because they don't know the priorities the boss has for shipping merchandise.

Wasted time occurs throughout the firm because the owner-manager is working beyond his capacity. The very elements that caused the firm to succeed may get buried in a mess of detail if the manager fails to establish the right systems and procedures at the right time.

The manager's unwillingness to add to overhead costs must be balanced against the advantages of establishing simple, easy to operate systems. For instance, suppose that each morning someone picks up the mail at a certain time, opens it, stamps the date, and separates and distributes it. Orders can then be directed to the proper person for sales or credit review, depending upon the established routine. Such a routine saves order processing time and aids in servicing the order more effectively.

What Is a Procedure? A procedure is a way of getting a routine job done with a minimum of confusion and waste. For example, the manager can set up a paperwork system so that a package will move routinely from the time a bill of lading is signed by a trucker to the time a customer's invoice is made out. Bills will get out faster, and the billing clerk will be more productive because of getting the information needed on time.

Only *nonroutine* matters should be called to the attention of the owner-manager or his key men (depending upon the established policies). A typical production order for a job-lot shop could be routinely processed as follows:

1. Sales—takes the order and clears it for credit.

2. Engineering—verifies product specifications and gives production a set of manufacturing instructions.

3. Production planning—reviews the order and orders the necessary parts from vendors; also notifies the customer of delivery status.

4. Production—makes the product according to production schedule and the customer's request.

5. Shipping—delivers according to schedule.

6. Office—invoices the customer and follows up on payment; files the original order for reference.

Only nonroutine problems affecting price, delivery date, or level of quality should be called to the attention of the owner-manager or appropriate supervisor.

Formality or complexity of paperwork will vary with the nature of a product and the size of a firm. As a firm grows, more of the employees become involved with turning out the product; thus, more and more people must know about all aspects of the order. The owner must see to it that the system and procedure for processing an order are understood by his employees. Further, once the system is installed and operating, no one should change or modify it unless all parties concerned are informed. Periodically, it is necessary to review the procedures and systems used, particularly if a firm is growing and/or changing its product lines or method of production.

The following areas (among others) require systems and procedures to help insure more effective production:

Inventory control.
Purchasing.
Job evaluation.
Merit rating.
Costs.
Production standards.
Quality control.
Receiving and shipping.
Tools, jigs, and fixtures.
Product engineering.
Sales data by product.

The owner-manager must determine the proper time for creating, installing, and using the right systems and procedures. If he acts too early, he will add unnecessarily to his costs. If he acts at the right time, he will have made a good investment.

Balancing "Doing" and "Managing"

As a firm develops and more people are employed, managerial problems increase, as does the time needed for solving them. The owner-manager must decide whether he will take on the added number of managerial responsibilities or whether he will continue as a "doer." As a doer he might work in the shop helping to design and build new jigs and fixtures, he might do machine setups, or he might even operate a group of machines himself. If he is an engineer, he may be so involved in designing an increasing number of orders that he has little time to attend to his managerial duties.

What Role Is To Be Played?

If the firm is to continue to grow successfully, the owner-manager must act. He must decide the role he will personally play in the growth of his enterprise. He must be able to assess:

1. The managerial needs of the firm.
2. His personal strengths and weaknesses in the managerial and technical needs of the business.
3. His personal interests in managing or doing.

Many owners of small firms have strong technical capacity but lack managerial training. The resulting frustrations of trying to develop technical innovations and, at the same time, trying to learn how to be a better manager can be very costly. In many cases, it would be wise to employ the services of the people needed to handle the increased managerial responsibilities. Within the firm itself might be someone who could be trained to handle part of the increased administrative burden.

Pat Anderson started a power supply business some years ago. He designed and built power equipment to the specifications of each customer. His unique ability to design compact units led to quick success for the firm. When Anderson Electronics received a growing number of orders, Pat hired two more engineers and began to involve himself deeply in production and general administrative problems. Before long, phone calls began coming in from a number of very unhappy customers; the power equipment they had received did not meet their rigorous specifications.

A number of other orders were in-process, and Pat held up many of the orders so that he could check out their engineering designs. As a result, delivery had to be delayed on a large amount of special material that Pat had purchased, and there was a sharp reduction in the amount of work available for the work force.

Anderson Electronics' earlier success had depended largely on the engineering skills of its owner-manager. Thus, there was not much merit to Pat's hiring additional engineers so that he could direct his efforts to overall managing. In too quickly giving the responsibility of designing to the new engineers, he left himself and his firm wide open to serious problems. He should have protected the firm's reputation for design more carefully. Pat might have hired one engineer and given him responsibility for designing—but only after his design skills had been proved.

The production responsibilities that Pat had assumed could have been handled by his foreman, or he might have hired a trained production manager. Such a man would have had some experience in setting up production standards, job evaluation reports, merit ratings, and a more formal system of production planning and control.

Pat's failure to analyze the importance of his own technical skills to the success of his firm was very costly. Although he recognized the production needs of the firm, his decision to direct them personally—without previous production management experience—left a very important base open and another base poorly covered.

The owner-manager must always be aware of how he is using his time. He must also have a clear understanding of his personal capabilities and limitations in the technical and managerial phases of his business. His job will change as the firm grows, but his role as a doer can be changed only if he has developed competent subordinates. The owner must judge the capabilities of his subordinates as he builds his organization. The more responsibility and authority they can assume, the greater amount of time he can spend on managing.

Guiding the Foreman

It is often said that a house is no stronger than its foundation. Likewise, a small manufacturing enterprise is no stronger than its foremen. The foremen are entrusted with the care and use of the firm's major assets. And they are the boss of the firm's production workers. The foreman represents the owner-manager as he directs the production workers in their daily activities. He is, in large measure, responsible for a worker's growth and development of skills. He is the person the operator looks to for personal direction. He is responsible for handling minor worker grievances. He determines which person will do which job, and when. He is responsible for the effective use of the firm's vital fixed assets: its real estate, specialized machinery, trucks, materials handling equipment and special jigs, and fixtures and tools.

The foreman also checks the daily use of material. In industries having high materials costs, this supervision involves responsibility for significant dollar amounts. And any good foreman must be able to carry out a given job using the methods established by management and keeping within the estimated labor and material costs.

The foreman in a small manufacturing enterprise controls the quantity and quality of production. And he is responsible for keeping his work force busy at all times. In many small firms, he is also the man who hires and fires and determines where and how many part-time employees will be employed.

Even when a firm grows and more formal routines for the management of the shop are installed, the foreman is still vital to success. The tasks he performs are many. He acts as adviser to the owner-manager and counselor to the workers, as inspector, training director, disciplinarian, and ambassador of good will, he is "the guy who knows how to put the product together," the one who is responsible for "getting the shipments out on time."

The Owner-Foreman Relationship. If developed properly, the relationship between owner and foreman enables the firm to maneuver quickly and gain an edge over its larger competitors. This is a challenging assignment for any owner-manager, but the firm that is built on a foundation of good foremen is well along the road to successful operation. Having unreliable foremen in a shop can be catastrophic.

It is vital for the owner-manager to understand the important role the foreman can and does play in the success of an enterprise. Unfortunately, too many owner managers equate the foreman's productivity and attitudes with their own rather than assessing them objectively. The foreman is expected to be a jack-of-all-trades throughout the shop rather than a specialist in a few functions. He is expected to be able to sit at the bench and produce the same quantity and quality of work as the full-time skilled operator. (This is important to many owner-managers in case someone skilled in a particular job quits or is out sick.) The manager expects the supervisor to be able to do everything that he himself knows how to do in the shop. But the owner must realize that the foreman probably lacks comparable background. When such an attitude is present in a small shop, hostility can develop between the owner-manager and his foremen, and growth of the firm can be seriously retarded.

Many times, a foreman will gain a sense of security by keeping details of machine setup and operation to himself. He reasons that as long as he alone knows the production secrets of the shop, the owner-manager cannot fire him. He is not interested in being a manager, but is content to be a doer. The firm cannot efficiently increase production in such a situation.

Avoid Needless Pressure. Sudden, needless pressure by an owner-manager often creates negative attitudes in his foremen; and the resulting confusion is easily communicated to everyone. The owner-manager must establish a positive plan that recognizes the limits of his supervisors' experience. He can only expect them to perform to reasonable standards. The foremen will probably have a more positive attitude toward their job and the firm than the average employee; but the owner-manager must recognize that his own motivations will almost surely exceed those of his foremen.

By employing his foremen within the limits of their background, experience, and skills, the owner-manager can reach higher levels of production. He will know how many foremen he will need at various levels, and his sense of timing in hiring or developing the necessary people will be improved. Depending upon the particular industry, product line, and skills involved, a nonworking foreman in a small shop can effectively supervise 15 to 25 workers. With one or two assistant foremen or keymen to do setups and some supervisory work, he should be able to supervise a greater number. A working-foreman—one who assigns work, sets up jobs, trains the operators, and checks the quality of the work produced, as well as performing certain operations at the bench himself—can supervise a maximum of 10 people.

The foreman, who is the vital link between the owner and the production force, plays a major part in the success or failure of a firm. The manager must decide how much responsibility and authority he aims to give his foremen and he should be very specific about how many dollars or units of production, he expects from each foreman's department each day, week, or month. If he spells out his wishes this way, the foreman will know when he is doing a good job and when he must call for help. Some owner managers feel that by not being specific or taking time to direct their foremen they will get more production from a department. They have the attitude "Let's get out all we can." This may work at times when the firm is very small and the manager is in the shop every day; but as the firm grows and more than two or three foremen work together, such a policy becomes less and less realistic.

Motivating Foremen. The owner manager should develop a plan to motivate his firstline foremen. One way to achieve higher levels of output and better quality is to set realistic production for each day, week, or month. The incentive to the foreman might be a cash bonus for exceeding the monthly output target while maintaining an acceptable level of product quality. As an alternative, particularly during weeks when the firm has a heavy backlog of orders, a bonus might be given for achieving 10 percent more than an average week's shipments. Another common financial incentive for foremen is the semiannual or annual bonus.

Often, the owner-manager can make very effective use of nonmonetary incentives. For example, he could:

1. Share certain types of confidential information with a foreman.

2. Permit a subordinate to help make an important decision.

3. Have a foreman represent the firm at trade shows or certain community meetings.

The owner's investment will be repaid many times over. By being highly motivated and better informed, the foreman will be more effective in his daily supervisory activities. And, knowing that, from time to time, he may be called on to participate in the affairs of the firm the highly motivated foreman would be certain to develop some understudy to "cover" for him. Consequently, he would become a more effective supervisor for the firm and also a more effective link between the owner-manager and the work force.

Summary

In the very competitive manufacturing community, only the firms that are creative, flexible, and continually seeking ways of improving productivity can survive. The owner-manager of a small firm faces competition from larger firms having bigger staffs; and yet, with a smaller organization and less capital, he must stay in business and grow. To do so, he must select the field where he can best use his unique skills. Serious problems are apt to result if he tries to compete in fields requiring large capital investments for machinery and equipment, in-depth technical organization, or a large national distribution organization.

On the other hand, he has an excellent opportunity to make money in firms requiring a unique process or skill knowhow, firms with the ability to move quickly in low capital investment, firms in seasonal industries with a style factor, or ones that are able to efficiently produce short-run- job-lot quantities of special products.

The owner-manager's approach to production in his firm can mean the difference between success and failure. As his firm grows, he must introduce certain tools of production management—such as product planning, plant layout, production methods, inspection and quality control. Nontechnical or administrative tools needed include production standards, incentive plans, job evaluations, merit ratings, and production control.

As his firm grows, the owner-manager must determine when to install these essential tools of production management. Once a system is introduced and is working, chances are its added expense will be balanced by more efficient production, cost savings, and better customer service.

To *use* these production tools, it will be necessary to set up a production *organization*. The owner-manager should start by reviewing his role in production as a "doer." Then he should begin developing his supervisory team. Supervisors may be "working foremen" or "full-time foremen," depending on the needs of a particular department or firm. Selection and training of production supervisors and the way in which the owner-manager subsequently works with them can spell the difference between a well-run shop and one that limps along. Foremen are the vital link between the owner-manager and the production force.

Chapter 3

SYSTEMS AND RECORDS

Good use of systems and records is an essential part of effective management. It is important to develop the appropriate systems, procedures, and records needed to implement a given policy. Records are important reporting devices that can help carry out a management policy.

The owner-manager must give careful thought to the systems and procedures that gather the information he uses in carrying out policies. And he should be aware of the importance of systems and procedures as management tools.

Using Systems and Records in the Small Firm

Business systems and procedures may be broadly termed "organized common sense." A formal definition might be: the organization of company policies, records, forms, and equipment in a manner that will help simplify and standardize business operations. The firm's activity—marketing, manufacturing, finance, or whatever—is performed by means of *routines* (systems and procedures) which translate the policies of the owner into action.

The Role of Systems, Procedures, and Records

A system is a series of steps planned to bring about a desired result. The steps themselves are the procedures that are used. Through the use of systems and procedures, a job or policy can be carried out with effectiveness and economy. Systems and procedures comprise more than just office and shop routines, accounting procedures, and new data processing methods, however. They can also be, and frequently are, the means by which broader policies of the owner-manager are translated into action.

Records can take various forms, depending on the nature of the business and the type of system. Their purpose is to document the significant facts for future use. For example, sales reports which analyze sales by area, product, and type of customers are helpful in making marketing decisions.

A system is a part of organization, not the whole of it. It helps bind the whole together; it assures that order and method will be used in all the operations of the business. When supervisors and operators follow a system, they will do their work and keep the necessary records according to an established procedure. If a regular and accustomed routine is used to handle key factors in a business such as salesmen's reports, receiving records, cash inflow, bill payments, employee grievance procedures, new personnel hiring, etc., then there will be no need to waste time and effort in repeating and checking preliminary steps in trying to find a solution to problems that arise.

The owner-manager can save himself a lot of valuable time if he will develop, install, and operate well-thought-out systems, procedures, and records. In the smaller firm, "it only takes a few minutes" to perform many of the operating functions, but as the firm grows, so does each of the operating functions, and a job that once was very minor can rapidly drain a large amount of the owner's time.

With a working program of systems, procedures, and records, an owner-manager can begin to operate according to the "exception principle" of management. That is, when employees understand systems and procedures and follow them as accepted practice, then the owner-manager is free to look after *exceptional* situations, knowing that accurate and up-to-date operating information will come from the systems he has set up.

Installing Systems and Records

In directing and controlling a company, regardless of its size or type, certain kinds of information are necessary. Current, or as current as possible, facts are needed on purchasing, inventory, production costs, overhead, and sales, to name a few.

In order to direct and control his firm effectively, the owner-manager must have information on each of the company's important activities. The data must enable him to maintain a balance among the various functions. Complete information concerning sales will not compensate for spotty information on production or finance. On many occasions the business facts required may be very simple. For example, in a shoe manufacturing firm having only six customers, all the information the owner-manager would need about them could be found in his sales journal and in a clip of unfilled orders arranged by customer. Note well, however, that the *simplicity of the situation would not eliminate the need for the information; it would only reduce the need for records.*

Kinds of Information Required

Typical kinds of information that may be required are as follows:

Sales. Facts and figures are needed on:

1. Summary of orders received.
2. List and condition of open orders.
3. Summary of sales and comparison with earlier records.
4. Analysis by area, product, and customer or type of customers.
5. Historical records for each customer, recognition of major customers.
6. List of potential customers.
7. Discount rates and terms for various customers.
8. Salesmen expense records, earnings, and percentage cost of sales for each salesman.

Production Control. The information should include:

1. Parts lists (with proper numbering system for products involving assembly).
2. Specification sheets.
3. Operation sheets.
4. Production schedules, general time schedule and/or machine loading or truck loading sheets.
5. Shop production orders (to describe job and accumulate costs).
6. Production progress sheets by job or parts.
7. Finished production reports.
8. Output of individual workers by hour, day, or week.

Warehouse and Shipping Control. This activity requires the following:

1. Receiving reports.
2. Receiving, placing into stock, production reports by packages and individuals.
3. Picking, packing, and shipping production reports.
4. Bills of lading and signed shipping documents.
5. Customer return report.
6. Backorder control documents.

Quality Control. The significant information is:

1. Proportion of rejections from receiving and production departments (scrap, seconds, and rework).
2. Reasons for rejections, internal and external.

Inventory Control. This type of information should include:

1. Amount of stock on hand (raw materials, goods in process, fabricated parts, finished goods, consigned goods).
2. Amounts on order (either production in shop or purchase orders).
3. Amounts allocated for certain jobs or customers.
4. Rate of parts or product usage and turnover.
5. Material requisitions.

Purchasing. Among the important items are:

1. Purchase requisitions, (vendor, receiving department, and office).
2. File of unfilled purchase orders.
3. List of suppliers, costs, and terms of past purchases.
4. File indicating when suppliers may have special offerings (important for retail, warehouse, and service industries).

Cost Accounting. Some of the signficant information to gather is:

1. Labor, material, and overhead costs for each product or job-lot.
2. Gross profit by item (applicable to certain retail and wholesale industries).

Finance and Credit. Included in this type of information is:

1. Monthly trial balance.
2. Financial statements (profit and loss and balance sheets).
3. Cash position.
4. Aging of accounts receivable and accounts payable.
5. Credit limits for customers and collection system.

Bookkeeping. The following are necessary.

1. Regular books of account: general ledger, accounts receivable ledger, accounts payable ledger, general journal, purchase journal, sales book, and cash book (or their equivalents).
2. Payroll information: pay checks, weekly payroll list, and individual annual earning statements.

The owner-manager of a small firm is rightfully concerned about the costs of designing, installing, and using written records. But he mustn't forget that records can help him control costs and manage more effectively. He will learn through experience how to balance the amount of recorded information necessary with the cost of securing it. He should not think that records will reduce the firm's flexibility and merely add to his overhead.

Where Systems Will Be Required

Before designing and installing records, the boss must consider their purpose and the particular system and procedure that will use the record. He must also know the capability of the employees who will be carrying out the system he establishes.

Systems and procedures will be needed in the following areas:

Office management.
Shop management.
Equipment standards.
Records management.
Office and shop appraisal.
Coordination.
Research and training.

The owner should review his office and shop management systems to see how well they apply the criteria of standardization, simplification, and production measurement. The systems should emphasize administrative work flows, organizational relationships established to process the work, and resulting records.

Equipment standards have to do with the review and testing of various makes and models of office machines and equipment to determine their proper use and economical operation. Because various procedures may require either manual or machine operations, the equipment program requires careful consideration. Given the continuing development of electronic computers and their increasing capability, the owner-manager should keep up to date on possible computer applications in his firm. In most cases, his first use of computers would be through an outside electronic data processing service bureau.

Records management is frequently handled very loosely in small firms. However, the alert owner-manager should give some thought to developing filing systems and time standards for filing by clerks. Records management also requires the arrangement, accessibility, and preservation of records in accordance with prescribed company policies.

Office and shop appraisal includes installing new methods and periodically reviewing existing records, systems, and procedures for effectiveness and usefulness. Appraisal would include comparative time measurements for work performed. The owner-manager should set up a systematic means of correlating forms and reports with related administrative procedures in other phases of the business and he should coordinate the dissemination of information. This will take time, but it is a necessary job.

Designing a System. When designing a system to accomplish a given management policy, the owner-manager must carefully consider the following:

1. Objectives and requirements of the system. What is it designed to accomplish? Is the fundamental requirement one of speed, of information, quality, or cost?
2. The people in the firm who will operate the system. How many people will be required and what background and skills will be needed?
3. Policies involved in the system. This will include pricing in a billing system, management's inventory policy in a material control system, and so on.
4. Details of the present system. This will seek to answer the questions who, what, when, where, why, and how.
5. Cost of the system. This will include number of people, equipment, records, forms, supplies, and space requirements.
6. Effectiveness of the system. Does it do what it is supposed to do in the time allowed, with the proper quality, at the lowest cost?
7. Interrelationship with other systems. Does the time study system unnecessarily complicate the payroll? Does the method of placing purchase orders multiply the work of accounts payable?
8. Forms, records and reports. Are they useful? Designed efficiently? Duplicate other documents? Properly filed? Retained for the proper period?

Because gathering such facts requires time, they should be carefully studied and used as the basis for a new program. The new program should:

1. Furnish adequate, accurate, and timely information.
2. Be simple to operate, economical to maintain, and sensitive to change.
3. Provide for "management by exception."
4. Help the owner-manager to plan ahead.

Mike Sherman's Allied Appliance Service Co. served the retail trade by repairing small radios and small home appliances in its downtown location. Large appliances such as refrigerators, washers, and TV sets were serviced by a fleet of three trucks. Mike operated one truck and employed servicemen for the other two. In the shop were two men, one handling the retail trade. The other did a number of jobs, including assigning jobs to the truck servicemen and purchasing supplies and parts. A bookkeeper came in once a week to make out the payroll, pay the bills, and send out statements.

When Mike Sherman attended a trade meeting he happened to talk with Dick Jones, who had an appliance

repair firm in the East. Jones, who was making more money than Mike on the same amount of business, said the two keys to his success were: (1) the way he charged for his firm's service (price being based upon a job's actual cost) and (2) the way he controlled his labor costs and his inventory of expensive parts and supplies. Mike decided to set up a system using (1) a weekly time report for the servicemen, and (2) a multipart snapout form consisting of a customer's invoice, a serviceman's cost control record, and an office control copy (see figure 3). The specific procedures for each step in the system were explained to the servicemen and the bookkeeper.

For the first few weeks, Mike spot-checked the servicemen's weekly time record each day when they were in the shop. He soon realized that one of the two trucks servicemen was very efficient but that the other was spending too much time on easy jobs and needed some training. (Later, Mike used the weekly time records as a basis for raises and bonuses.) Because he operated the third service truck, Mike also filled in a report, and, as a result, recognized some ways in which he could improve his own performance.

The multipart job ticket was put into use about 4 weeks after the weekly time report was instituted. Each job ticket was numbered and when a job was assigned to a man, the job ticket was put on a clipboard assigned to each man. The office copy was filed in numerical order. Thus, Mike could quickly note the total number of jobs received on a given day, where they were located, and the promises given to the customer for service.

The men complained about posting on the invoice the parts used in making repairs, so Mike decided that jobs billed for less than $15 did not require parts posting. The men received some complaints from customers that charges were high, so Mike studied the situation and made changes in labor charges. At the end of the first month, billings had increased more than 10 percent, and at the end of the second month, by 20 percent.

As part of the control of materials, it was necessary for Mike to take weekly parts inventories of the service trucks. The all-around man in the shop kept a running inventory card on each truck. He noted (at cost) what was issued and then, once each week, using customer job-tickets, deducted the materials billed out. He made adjustments for jobs in-process each week when he took the truck inventories of each man. Minor discrepancies noted right after the installation of the materials control system soon settled down to negligible amounts. Mike was very satisfied with his newly developed systems, procedures, and records because they gave him the control he was looking for and at the same time led to higher profits.

Although Mike's informal approach to establishing the systems and procedures was very effective, the owner-manager of a larger (or growing) firm would find it advisable to put the procedures in writing. As an owner-manager withdraws from personal, daily participation in a phase of his business, he must rely more heavily on the information the systems generate.

Recordkeeping Forms

The printed form is the basis of good records and effective systems. It is the primary record of the status of an operation, and the only one other than memory. The increasing use of electronic data processing will have an important effect on systems in small firms.

Some of the common types of forms are letterheads, time cards, employment applications, and payroll checks; more complex types include manufacturing orders, bills of material, operation sheets, etc. Certain useful documents—such as advertising circulars, product labels, price lists, and customer instruction sheets—are really not forms. But any printed document that is an essential link in an operating procedure or is a medium for business communication should be considered a form.

Developing the Right Form. Forms are usually developed for the following purposes: to acknowledge, to agree, to apply, to authorize, to cancel, to certify, to claim, to estimate, to follow up, to identify, to instruct, to notify, to order, to record, to report, to request, to route, and to schedule.

Determining whether a form is needed for one of these purposes is the owner-manager's responsibility. He should review records currently in use and determine how additional ones would fit in. He should study the function the form or record is to serve, the number of transactions expected in a given period of time, and the number and duties of those who will use the form. And he should follow the use of the record from inception through disposition (filed, attached to something, or thrown away).

Thought must be given at the outset to the development of forms. Once a record is installed, it is difficult to eliminate and costly of staff time. And forms, themselves, also cost money to set up and print.

Changing policies in a firm will require corresponding changes in systems and procedures. And these may, in turn, require changes in the design of forms or number of copies needed of certain ones. Because the records needs of a small

Figure 3

Mike Sherman's Systems and Procedures

OBJECTIVES: To establish the price charged for service on the basis of actual material used and time spent.
To control the time of the three outside servicemen.
To control the parts and supplies inventory.

SYSTEM: Serviceman's Weekly Time Report

Issued by office, weekly
Posted daily by serviceman
Returned to office on Saturdays
Used by bookkeeper to prepare payroll, weekly
Studied by owner for time use and billings for each man
Filed by servicemen

PROCEDURES:

Detailed procedures for each operation were described orally to each serviceman.

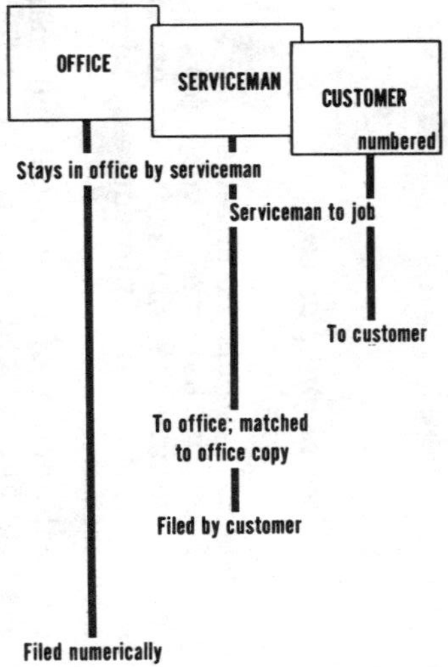

Customer Job Ticket and Invoice

Customers call; job ticket filled out in office
- Assigned to a service man
- Serviceman requisitions parts
- Parts cost noted on invoice

Serviceman does the job
- Notes time on job
- Calculates labor, material costs
- Gives customer invoice
- Gets paid
- Turns in serviceman's copy with money to office

Office puts service copy together with office copy
- Calculates invoice as a check
- Reconciles cash
- Notes materials used by serviceman
- Files invoice copies one by customer and one by number

firm are continually changing, it is best, when possible, to design forms having some flexibility. Actual layout requires the skill of an experienced forms designer, who can also select the right printing process, paper, carbon, and quantities. Inventory control of forms is usually delegated to someone in the office. Forms, as the basis for records, are very important in the execution of the firm's policies, but some balance must be kept to avoid duplication and waste.

The Value of Records and Systems Management

Every business has certain basic policies—whether they are written or only kept in mind by the owner. Policies are a management control that must be followed. Many times, the thought and planning involved in a firm's records and systems will determine the successful execution of the owner-manager's policies.

Merits of Records and Systems

Records and systems management is an integral part of the job of every manager. Every person who supervises, directs, or administers the activities of subordinates is responsible for the systems, procedures, and records that he and his employees use.

The initial impulse of most small firm managers is to think that systems and procedures are a tool for the use of large firms only. The necessary paperwork and equipment make them costly to develop, and the time required for development and introduction in the firm make them costly to execute. The cost of staff time is another factor; in some cases, owner-managers expect their key subordinates to do paperwork in the evenings or on weekends at home.

Some small firm owner-manager's recognize the value of establishing a records and systems program. They set up a program related to the size of their firm. Systems can be as simple as one-page memos, supplemented by oral directions. As the firm grows, and more managers and operators are employed, the systems and procedures program will become more formal.

Alan Karl owned and managed the 90-year-old Karl Jewelry Co. The firm made a line of costume jewelry which sold very successfully in department stores and discount chains throughout the country. The firm's

major problem was how to increase production enough to keep up with a 30 to 40 percent yearly increase in business.

Shipments seemed to have reached a level regardless of the overtime used or the number of people employed; as a result, many orders with potentially high profits had to be added to the backlog. Alan had hired a new plant manager, but this only seemed to have created more problems. The old-time foremen, who had been instrumental a year earlier in getting another experienced plant manager fired, didn't cooperate with the new plant manager. And Alan contributed, to some extent, to his production problem. In daily visits to each department, he was forever critical of various operators who might be walking around or talking to fellow workers. He was always griping in public to his foremen about their lack of production when so many orders were in the house. Yet, the foremen worked very hard. They put in very long hours—in some cases as many as 70 hours a week—for long periods of time. Some of their time was spent working at the bench. There was a real effort to get orders produced, but somehow the plant did not keep up with sales.

Alan called in a consultant experienced in production problems who studied the systems, procedures, and records used in processing an order from arrival to shipment. He found a great deal of confusion at many points. With the existing routines and records, there was no way to control the flow of work through the shop. Many of the foremen operated their departments without direction. They had a few systems, procedures, and records, but hardly enough to operate their departments effectively.

Alan and the consultant, after lengthy discussion, developed a plan to add new procedures and adapt those already in use. And Alan agreed with the consultant that he should stay out of the shop and let the plant manager be the boss.

The consultant formed a foreman team which met once a week. The foremen met together with the consultant to discuss the new routines and proposed records that were to be installed. Each foreman knew that every morning by 10:00 he was to have reported his previous day's production to Mr. Karl. A man was added to control the flow of work between departments. Mr. Karl and the consultant worked out each system and record that was to be used in the shop. They checked the operation of the system very closely at the beginning. As they went on to new systems, the old ones were checked periodically or whenever a problem developed.

Within 6 months, productivity increased appreciably. Mr. Karl received his daily production information and

concentrated on getting more sales and developing new products. Without Mr. Karl's daily tours of the shop, the plant manager was able to establish good working relationships with the foremen and help them do a more productive job.

The future growth of Karl Jewelry was made possible when Mr. Karl withdrew from the shop and concentrated on reviewing all phases of the firm's order processing and production. He was able to study every system, procedure, and record used in the shop and was effective in installing new routines. Also, with the help of the consultant and plant manager, he was able to train his foreman in the new, more effective routines. He was able to delegate, with confidence, the manufacturing responsibility and authority to his new plant manager, and could rely on the new system to give him the necessary production information. He was able to use his skills more effectively in sales and product development, and thus provide new business opportunities for his firm.

Handling Problems Without Systems and Procedures

Many small business owner-managers make decisions at a very fast pace. Is all this speed and rush necessary? Although the small firm owner-manager must be able to move quickly, must he "do" everything? In a one-man firm, nothing can be delegated, but when employees are hired the owner-manager should decide which projects he can delegate. As more people are added to the firm, further decisions will be needed concerning duties each person will perform.

If the owner-manager understands the function of systems and records in his firm, he can make more effective use of his employees' time and experience. If he is unable to discipline himself to use systems, procedures, and records in his firm, he may face some of the following problems:

1. Lack of time to complete all the necessary projects in the shop.
2. Lack of time to spend with his family.
3. Wasted time by employees because they have not been trained to perform their jobs according to established policies, systems, and procedures.
4. Lack of information on employees' productivity, which may result in unfair pressure on them.
5. Poor decisions based on inaccurate and invalid information.
6. Inability to build organization owing to lack of development and assistance of key men.
7. Unrest and reduced operator efficiency owing to lack of strong supervisory group.

8. Inability of the firm to move quickly because the owner-manager is enmeshed in too many details.

Owner-Manager's Responsibilities

The owner-manager must make most decisions at a moment's notice. Regardless of what they relate to, these decisions should be based on accurate, up-to-the-minute operating information.

As a company's size and operations grow, its owner-manager's need for accurate, current data becomes even more pressing. In a firm having three employees, the owner-manager can personally get the facts in all phases of his business; but in a 30-man firm, the owner has to rely on information and records gathered by his staff.

To make good decisions, the owner-manager must develop and analyze pertinent facts. After considering past and present facts, he should also examine the effects of various alternatives and perhaps develop a forecast based upon the alternatives. His ultimate decision should result from the analysis he makes of the facts he gathers, weighed together with any previous experience in the particular problem being considered.

The owner-manager must decide when a system or a record is required to develop information for a specific problem. He must also decide whether the time and funds invested in gathering certain data are worthwhile.

Milton Lambert owned and managed a rapidly expanding food product firm, Lambert Fine Foods, Inc. His sales staff, calling on independent supermarkets, chains, and wholesalers, had grown from 5 to 20 persons in a 2-year period. Lambert's oldest and most successful salesman, though dubbed field sales manager, actually directed only 5 men in a small area around the headquarters, and Lambert, himself, by phone and occasional personal visits, directed the others.

The five nearby salesmen were closely managed, but the others got little direction and supervision and had no records to maintain. In time, Lambert realized that his expanded sales force was proportionally less effiective than the smaller one he had directed before his firm began to grow. His position was clearly brought home by the news from his accountant that the firm's cost of selling had increased more than 25 percent in the past year.

After a careful survey of the situation, Lambert decided to hire a sales administrator to handle all internal matters for his sales force. This would relieve the field sales manager of a number of details and would allow him to assist Lambert in directing, training, and controlling the entire sales force.

This new program required a number of new systems, procedures, and records to improve communication between the salesmen, the field sales manager, and Mr. Lambert. The new sales administrator developed systems and reports that included information about each salesman's itinerary, calls, costs, and performance.

Within 3 months, the new program of salesman direction and control was in effect. Performance of some of the salesmen stepped up immediately. They realized that Lambert now would have better control and that if they wanted to stay with the firm they had better improve their performance.

As a result of the information the new system produced, Lambert readjusted certain territories and changed some salesmen from one territory to another. Sales continued to rise, as did the effectiveness of the sales force. In time, more salesmen were hired and the firm continued to expand.

Lambert went through some unnecessary bumps in his field sales operations. While his firm was expanding, he should have been modifying his organization so that he could have sustained more effective direction and control. Luckily, he was able to recognize his problem before it became too acute.

Maintaining Records and Systems

Constant change placed teriffic pressure on the various systems, procedures, and records of a firm. Many owner-managers say, "We'll take care of the system or report later; we don't have time now." From that moment on, confusion and wasted managerial effort begin. Take, for example, the case of the Jackson Drug Co.:

John Jackson, who owned one drug store, bought a second one in the same town. About 6 months later, he began to receive letters and phone calls from his suppliers complaining about not being paid the proper amounts. On checking with the manager of the new store, John realized that he had failed to specify any procedures for receiving goods and keeping records of them when he had bought the new store. John also found that he had little or no control of goods being transferred

between the stores. He hadn't developed a profit-and-loss statement since buying the second store, and he realized that without a receiving system or adequate record-keeping, he had no way of knowing how the new store was doing.

John Jackson was exposed to many business risks because he didn't maintain the necessary systems and records in his second store. He recognized their importance in his first store, where he personally saw to it that his staff keep accurate and up-to-date records. But in buying the new store, he neglected to develop the necessary systems. Jackson's error was a common one. Despite their importance, records and systems management often fail to receive proper attention from the small business owner-manager.

As the preceding case illustrates, the growing small firm can be strongly affected by changes; among these are the following:

1. Addition of new people in office, shop, or sales force.
2. Changes in products or service (particularly design and production).
3. Addition of a new facility.
4. Appointment of new supervisors.
5. Rise in sales (causing greater activity throughout the firm).

When he adds new people to the firm or changes the jobs of present employees, the owner-manager must train them to use the existing systems without variation—unless he gives specific consent.

Existing systems and records may become obsolete as the firm grows and the number and types of transactions increase. If they do, the owner-manager must develop an orderly way to handle the necessary changes. The development and installation of new or modified systems and records in the firm should not be taken lightly by anyone in the organization.

Summary

The owner-manager of a growing small firm should be aware of the importance of records and systems as a management tool that can help put his operating policies into action. A progressive small firm can attract and hold qualified employees if they have a genuine opportunity to do their job. Using systems and records as a tool of action and as an instrument of control helps the owner-manager develop the abilities of his key subordinates. Records that measure performance will help the owner-manager know what is going on, and he will be more willing to delegate the authority necessary for his key men to perform. Delegation allows the owner/manager to keep out of day-to-day, routine problems, and to concentrate on handling exceptional problems.

As his firm grows, the owner-manager's approach to systems must change from giving simple oral directions to using a more formal written program. More detailed systems, procedures, and records are necessary because the owner-manager will not have time to do all tasks himself. He will have to rely on the up-to-date, accurate information developed from the systems and operating procedures he establishes. The effectiveness of his decisions will depend on the information and records his organization generates. He should periodically audit his systems to assure that the information coming from them is accurate, and also make the necessary changes as the firm grows and policies change. Typically, recordkeeping for historical purposes gradually shifts to records for communication and planning.

The effective manager must develop systems and records that will help him make the most efficient use of his and his staff's time. He will need to be up to date on the current methods of data processing, and aware of the types of systems, procedures, and records used in his industry. He will also need to update his staff's managerial skills. His reward will be in the form of extra time gained for managing—and the resulting opportunity to achieve the goals he has set for himself and his business.

Chapter 4

FINANCIAL MANAGEMENT

MANY owner-managers of small firms try to expand and earn increasing profits on a very thin investment. To succeed, it is important to have or develop skills in financial management. As an owner-manager improves his financial skills, he must also invest the necessary time in financial planning and control of his business. In a small firm, financial information is probably more vital than it is in a larger one, and yet takes less time to generate.

Financial skills should include understanding of the balance sheet, the profit-and-loss statement, cash flow projection, break-even analysis, and source and application of funds, all of which are discussed in the following pages. Lack of adequate working capital is usually the greatest weakness of the small firm. In many firms, husband and wife run the business; it is especially important that both of them understand financial management.

Tools of Financial Management

Most small business owners are not accountants, but they must understand the tools of financial management if they are going to be able to measure the return on their investment. The owner-manager doesn't need to know the precise meanings of the items in his balance sheet and profit-and-loss statement, but he must be able to interpret these records accurately.

The owner-manager can develop his understanding of the tools of financial management with the aid of his accountant, lawyer, banker, or perhaps the credit manager of a major supplier. Responsibilities to himself and to others make it imperative that he be acquainted with the function and purpose of the balance sheet and income statement.

The immediate cause of many business failures is inability to pay debts as they come due, but underlying causes may be weaknesses in sales or operations, inadequate working capital, losses from pilferage, or other reasons. Using the tools of financial management, either by himself or with outside assistance, the owner-manager may be able to detect beforehand those problems which could bring on bankruptcy.

Although good records are essential to good financial management, they alone are not enough because their full use requires interpretation and analysis. The owner-manager's financial decisions concerning return on invested funds, approaches to banks, securing greater supplier credit, raising additional equity capital, and so forth, can be more successful if he takes the time to develop understanding and use of the balance sheet and profit-and-loss statement.

Balance Sheets and Derived Ratios

The balance sheet shows the financial condition of a firm at the end of business on a specific day. It is called a balance sheet because total assets balance with, or are equal to, total liabilities plus net worth (see figure 4 for a concise balance sheet). Balance sheets are compiled monthly, quarterly, semiannually, and/or yearly depending upon the needs of a firm. Unaudited balance sheets developed between regular compilation dates can also be a valuable management tool.

Assets are listed in order of their convertibility into cash. Those considered convertible within 1 year are called current assets and are totaled in the first part of the asset column—

"above the line" in banking and credit terminology. Current liabilities, those due within 1 year, are listed similarly, at the top of the liabilities. Subtracting total liabilites from total assets gives net worth or ownership equity. Subtracting current liabilities from current assets gives working capital or net current assets. Quick assets are those which, as the name implies, can be almost immediately converted into cash. Too much should not be tied up in fixed assets when compared with current assets and/or net worth.

Asset Accounts

Some of the asset accounts may be described as follows:

CASH—Total cash *in bank* (Every business, however small, needs *a cash journal* of some sort, not just the balance as shown in a firm's checkbook) plus petty cash in the office. Frequently, because of outstanding checks, a firm has more funds available in the bank than its checkbook shows. These funds should not be used, however.

NOTES AND ACCOUNTS RECEIVABLE—Represents amounts due the company, usually from customers, within a period of one year or less on notes and open accounts known to be collectable. Notes and accounts receivable may also be due from the owner-manager, stockholders, etc.

INVENTORY—The stocks of materials, supplies, and finished goods of retailers, wholesalers, and manufacturers. The manufacturer has raw materials, work-in-process, finished goods, and sometimes consigned goods. Finished goods are merchandise ready for sale; they are often warehoused and used as a basis for borrowing.

All inventories should be valued according to an accepted method; the one generally used is "cost or market, whichever is lower." Whenever taking physical inventories, the owner-manager must be careful to obtain accurate counts and descriptions of all items. Pricing, extensions, and footings should be accurate. To avoid errors, each of the sheets used in taking the inventory should be numbered.

In considering a loan to a small business, banks are likely to place particular emphasis on the fixed assets and their liquidating value shown on the balance sheet.

PROPERTY—Includes land and buildings. The value indicated should be the cost of acquisition. If land value has appreciated, the bank should give separate consideration to value of land and buildings. Any buildings owned will be shown on the balance sheet at cost less depreciation, computed at the appropriate rate.

EQUIPMENT—Should be valued at cost less an allowance for depreciation and/or obsolescence.

MACHINERY—Should be handled on the same basis as equipment.

Mortgages on any of the preceding should be indicated, so that a complete picture of each item is available.

Figure 4—Balance Sheet for the Wheeler Company

Assets:	Dec. 31 Prior year	Dec. 31 Last year	Change
Cash	$ 140	$ 605	+$ 465
Accounts receivable (net)	$ 44,690	$ 34,890	−$ 9,800
Inventory	$ 70,700	$109,770	+$39,070
TOTAL CURRENT ASSETS	$115,530	$145,265	
Property and Machinery (Net of Depreciation)	$ 23,810	$ 55,715	+$31,905
TOTAL	$139,340	$200,980	+$61,640
Liabilities and Net Worth			
Short Term Notes	....	$ 20,000	+$20,000
Accounts payable	$ 68,340	$ 86,720	+$18,380
Taxes payable (State, Local, & Federal)	$ 11,720	$ 14,880	+$ 3,160
TOTAL CURRENT LIABILITIES	$ 80,060	$121,600	
NET WORTH	$ 59,280	$ 79,380	+$20,100
TOTAL	$139,340	$200,980	+$61,640

Liability and Net Worth Accounts

Liability and net worth accounts may be described as follows:

NOTES PAYABLE—Amount of notes signed for borrowing purposes; may include notes owed to banks, supplier firms, or individuals.

ACCOUNTS PAYABLE—Total amounts owed to trade creditors for merchandise, materials, and supplies. If dating terms are given, they would also be included.

ACCRUED LIABILITIES—Unrecorded expenses incurred at the close of the fiscal or calendar year are current liabilities. Such items as wages, salaries, taxes, and interest accrued are often omitted from balance sheets, either through oversight or intentionally. Failure to *include them* results in an understatement of liabilities and overstatement of both working capital and net worth. Dividends declared by the board of directors, payable on a given date, similarly represent a liability of the corporation and should be shown among current liabilities with the date of payment.

TAXES PAYABLE—Local, State, and Federal taxes; They should be estimated and included among current liabilities.

FUNDED DEBT—Serial bonds, notes on mortgage installments, mortgages, and other funded debts due and payable within one year are current liabilities. Segregation of these amounts is needed for determining the current ratio and working capital position of the company.

DEFERRED INCOME—This item represents monies received but not yet earned. Ordinarily, that portion of the income which has been earned is included in the profit and loss statement and the unearned portion is shown as an item of deferred income in the liability section of the balance sheet. Failure to set up the unearned portion as a liability results in an overstatement of liabilities.

CONTINGENT LIABILITIES—Disclosure of contingent liabilities is essential in determining the prospective financial condition and current position of a company. Failure to disclose them in the balance sheet or profit-and-loss statement prohibits due consideration in any credit or investment analysis.

NET WORTH—Net worth is the total assets of the firm less the total liabilities. In a corporation, it includes both capital stock and surplus.

CAPITAL STOCK is the total value of shares issued to the owner of the business. If the firm is unincorporated, there will be no capital stock account. Instead, capital accounts will appear under the name(s) of the owner(s), showing how much equity the owners have in the business.

Generally speaking, *surplus* is of two major kinds, earned and capital. Earned surplus arises out of undistributed earnings and is defined as the balance of net profits, income and gains of a corporation from the date of incorporation after deducting losses and after deducting distributions to stockholders and transfers to capital stock accounts when made out of such surplus. An unincorporated business does not have a surplus account.

In addition, the balance sheet can show *intangible assets*. Under this classification are included such items as patents, trade-marks, copyrights, franchises, goodwill, and other intangibles. Such intangibles are shown in the balance sheet usually at arbitrary values established by management. For most analysis purposes, intangibles are deducted from net worth. Valuation of intangibles can be distorted by failure to provide adequate reserves for amortization and by overstatement or understatement of the periodic amortization charges.

Another item that should be considered is *deferred charges.* This caption includes such things as unamortized debt discounts and expenses, experiment costs, discounts and commissions on capital stock, and other deferred expenses. Ordinarily, these items are written off to current operations or amortized over a period of years. Failure to charge the consumed or expired portion of deferred items to operations results in an overstatement of both assets and net worth.

The owner-manager should not look upon the preparation of the balance sheet as a burden; nor should he fail to use it as a source for management guidance. If he is going to stay in business, he must have a reasonable knowledge of the tools of financial management. After looking at a balance-sheet statement, he should be able to assess the general state of a firm's health. By inspecting a number of statements for consecutive accounting periods, he should be able to see the general financial trend of the firm. He should study financial management, either books (see the references, at the end of this chapter) or as a student in one of the many courses on finance periodically offered by universities, colleges, trade associations, and business organizations.

Financial Ratios

The owner-manager needs some way of comparing the performance of his company with another or with industry averages. Ratios are the tool for this. There are three kinds: Balance sheet ratios show the relationships between various balance sheet items. Operating ratios show the relationships of expense accounts to income. The third kind shows the relationship between an item on the profit-and-loss statement and one on the balance sheet.

As a practical illustration of the use of selected financial ratios, consider the Wheeler Company (figure 5). The owner-manager's comparison of last year's ratios with the year before that indicates areas of financial improvement or weakening. An analysis of Wheeler's performance reveals the following:

CURRENT RATIO—The firm's current ratio weakened from 1.44 to 1.19 because of large increases of property and machinery. This lower ratio reduced its ability to generate cash.

QUICK RATIO—Wheeler's increased inventory weakened its ability to raise cash; the quick ratio dropped from .56 to .29, or almost 50 percent.

ACCOUNTS RECEIVABLE TURNOVER—The increase from 10.7 to 16.9 indicates that receivables "turned" to sales a greater number of times. This is a good sign. Management should try to determine the factors responsible for the improvement.

ACCOUNTS RECEIVABLE OUTSTANDING (AVERAGE DAYS)—The reduction from 33.6 days to 21.3 indicates an improvement in customer payments—perhaps the result of management's increased credit and collection activities. Quicker collection of accounts will tie up less capital as the firm continues to grow.

INVENTORY TURNOVER—Wheeler Company's increase in inventory from $70,700 to $109,770 caused a slowdown in its turnover ratio. The ratio of the number of times Wheeler's inventory turned over fell from 5.7 in the prior year to 4.7 in the last year. This ratio is vital for small business owner-managers, who must make most effective use of the limited capital available to them. In general, the higher the inventory turnover, the more successful the manager's performance.

OPERATING PROFIT PERCENTAGE—The reduction in operating profit from 9.4 percent to 6.4 percent is a matter for serious management analysis.

NET PROFIT PERCENTAGE—The increase in Wheeler's interest payments and in "other deductions" caused the net profit percentage to decrease from 6.2 percent to 4.2 percent. This drop requires immediate management action.

RETURN ON INVESTMENT—The ratio of net profit to net worth shows exactly what the business earned on the equity capital invested. Of course, in many cases, the owner must develop an "*adjusted* net profit to net worth ratio." He must take into consideration personal salary drawings that may be greater than nominal, and he must consider any abnormal personal expenses. On the other hand, net worth, as stated, may actually reflect a very conservative inventory policy. Borderline items classed as expenses, instead of capitalized, will also cause book net worth to appear low. The effects on "true return on investment" can be considerable. The owner-manager may think he is doing well with the funds he has "invested," but, in fact, he may be doing poorly when he takes all factors into proper account.

DEBT TO NET WORTH—The total debt of the Wheeler Company increased from $80,060 to $121,600, raising the debt to net worth ratio from 1.35 to 1.53. This increase is a signal to management to restrain its purchases of inventory, property, and machinery.

Figure 5—Selected Financial Ratios From The Wheeler Company's Balance Sheet

Ratio	Formula	Dec. 31 Prior year		Dec. 31 Last year	
Current Ratio (Times)	Cash, Accounts Receivable, Inventory / Accounts payable & taxes payable	$115,530 / $ 80,060	=1.44	$145,265 / $121,600	=1.19
Quick Ratio (Times)	Cash & Accounts Receivable / Accounts payable & taxes payable	$ 44,830 / $ 80,060	= .56	$ 35,495 / $121,600	= .29
Accounts Receivable Turnover (Times)	Sales / Accounts Receivable	$480,115 / $ 44,690	=10.7	$589,480 / $ 34,890	=16.9
Average Days Accounts Receivable and Outstanding	Days in Year / Accounts receivable turnover	360 / 10.7	=33.6	360 / 16.9	=21.3

Inventory Turnover (Times)	Cost of Goods / Inventory	\$400,985 / \$ 70,700	=5.7	\$515,300 / \$109,770	=4.7
Operating Profit (Percentage)	Operating Profit / Sales	\$ 45,080 / \$480,115	=9.4	\$ 37,790 / \$589,480	=6.4
Net Profit (Percentage)	Net Profit / Sales	\$ 30,000 / \$480,115	=6.2	\$ 24,670 / \$589,480	=4.2
Return on Investment (Percentage)	Net Profit / Net Worth	\$ 30,000 / \$ 59,280	=50.6	\$ 24,670 / \$ 79,380	=31
Debt to Net Worth (Percentage)	Accounts payable, Taxes payable / Net Worth	\$ 80,060 / \$ 59,280	=1.35	\$121,600 / \$ 79,380	=1.53

In addition to the analysis of the balance sheet ratios developed, the owner-manager will find it valuable to compare his firm's ratios with those of other companies in the same industry. Sources for such ratios include Dun & Bradstreet, Robert Morris Associates (The National Association of Bank Loan Officers), trade associations, trade publications, universities, and public accounting firms.

Profit-and-Loss (Operating) Statement

The owner-manager must have some gage to measure the degree of success or failure of his business. He must know the net result of subtracting expenses from earnings. The profit-and-loss statement is the gage used to determine profitability. Unlike the balance sheet, which shows the condition of a firm *at a given moment,* it measures the profit or loss of a firm over a period of time—a month, quarter, or year, for example.

The use of monthly operating figures derived from the monthly trial balance is a necessity, *regardless* of the size of the firm. The owner-manager need not take a physical inventory each month in order to have a profit-and-loss statement. His accountant can develop the statement by using various methods to arrive at the cost of goods sold. The monthly profit-and-loss statement should be in the hands of the manager by the end of the second week of the following month if it is to be of value in determining areas of strength and weakness in the business. To accomplish this, the bookkeeper and other members of the firm must stay up to date on all accounting and control matters. Suppliers usually send in invoices on time; receiving records must be sent to the bookkeeper on time; and so forth.

The monthly profit-and-loss statement and balance sheet are also useful for verification of the accuracy and completeness of the daily and weekly financial and operating information that the owner-manager relies on in making his day-to-day decisions.

Amount of Detail Needed

The detail needed for the accounts on the profit-and-loss statement will vary with the type and size of firm. Enough detail should be included to enable the owner-manager to determine *where* he is earning gross profit and *how* he is spending money. For example, a retailer of home furnishings and appliances might set up two gross profit accounts because the two product lines would show wide variation in gross profits. Yet, it might be best to keep the expense records together (in one account) because of the common use of the firm's showroom, warehouse, and delivery trucks. Similarly, many manufacturers handle products "for resale only" in addition to their normal manufacturing operations. In such situations, it might be advisable to keep a separate accounting of the gross profits earned from the two different activities.

Wheeler's Yearly P&L Statement

The Wheeler Company is a typical job-lot manufacturer; a description of the principal items in its profit-and-loss statement (see figure 6) follows:

1. NET SALES—Represents gross dollar sales minus merchandise returns and allowances. Some accountants also deduct cash discounts granted to customers, saying that these actually reduce the net selling price; others credit the discount to "other expenses." "Trade" and "quantity" discounts are concessions off price and should be deducted from gross sales. Out-freight is also a deduction if goods are sold f.o.b. destination. In setting up profit-and-loss statements in percentages, net sales are shown as 100 percent.

2. COST-OF-GOODS SOLD—Consists of direct materials consumed in the period, direct labor, and shop overhead. Shop overhead includes indirect labor, machinery repairs, light, heat, power, insurance, factory supplies, rent, depreciation, and plant supervisory salaries. All items except direct materials consumed can be accurately and completely accumulated. The materials consumed figure is determined by adding purchases and incoming freight to the beginning inventory and then subtracting the ending inventory.

The accuracy of this account depends upon the care used in measuring the beginning and ending inventories. This account affects the valuation of the gross profit for the period and hence the entire profit-and-loss statement.

The owner-manager's participation in inventory-taking is essential. He must understand the condition, quantities, and values of his inventory in order to interpret the profit-and-loss statement. He must make certain that each inventory count is taken in a consistent fashion—from raw materials through work-in-process to finished goods. Otherwise, the materials used figure won't be accurate. If the inventory is consistent, he will then be in a position to judge material usage and how it relates to the product mixture of sales and to his method of estimating and pricing business.

For retailers and wholesalers, the cost of goods figure includes the beginning inventory plus purchases and freight-in during the period covered, *minus* the ending inventory. Retailers and wholesalers need even greater accuracy than manufacturers when they take inventory because a larger proportion of their capital is tied up. It is very difficult not to be overstocked on at least some slow-moving items.

Figure 6—Comparison of 12-Months Profit and Loss

	Dec. 31 Prior year	Percent	Dec. 31 Last year	Percent
1. NET SALES	$480,115	100	$589,480	100
2. COST OF GOODS SOLD (Direct materials, direct labor, and shop overhead)	$400,985		$515,300	
3. GROSS PROFIT	$ 79,130	16.5	$ 74,180	12.8
4. Other Operating Expenses (Sales overhead, administration overhead, & general overhead)	$ 34,050	7.1	$ 36,390	6.2
5. OPERATING PROFIT	$ 45,080	9.4	$ 37,790	6.6
6. Interest and other deductions	$ 1,030		$ 1,600	
7. PROFIT BEFORE TAXES	$ 44,050	9.2	$ 36,190	6.2
8. Taxes	$ 14,050		$ 11,520	
9. NET PROFIT	$ 30,000	6.2	$ 24,670	4.2
10. Dividends	$ 10,000		$ 4,000	
11. Retained in the business	$ 20,000		$ 20,670	

3. GROSS PROFIT—Determined by deducting cost of goods from net sales. This is an important figure, particularly when competition forces prices down. Increases and decreases in prices can have a great effect both on gross profit dollars and on gross profit percentage. A slight reduction in price may require a substantial increase in volume if the same amount of gross profit dollars is to be realized.

4. OTHER OPERATING EXPENSES—Includes selling, administrative, and general expenses. Additional classifications may be established depending upon the size of the firm, the nature of the industry, and the wishes of the owner-manager.

Selling overhead includes salesmen's salaries or commissions, sales executives' wages, sales office salaries, travel expenses, trade show expenses, entertainment, sales promotion, and advertising. The ratio of selling overhead to net sales should be reviewed and controlled often.

Administrative overhead includes administrative or office salaries and wages, light, heat, communications, cost of legal and accounting services, etc. General expenses include unusual expenses not classified elsewhere.

5. OPERATING PROFIT—The difference between gross profit on sales and operating expenses. Operating profit measures the effectiveness of management operations for a period of time. The owner-manager should always watch the ratio of operating profit to sales because it reflects the overall effectiveness of his decisions.

6. INTEREST AND OTHER DEDUCTIONS—Includes interest, doubtful accounts, and discounts granted (if not already deducted from sales). Also included are unusual costs such as losses on the sale of fixtures or machinery.

7. PROFIT BEFORE TAXES—The profit achieved by a firm when interest expense and other deductions have been deducted from the operating profit.

8. TAXES—Federal, State, and local taxes due or paid by the firm out of its earnings. Special conditions allow the elimination or reduction of taxes for certain periods—for example, previous losses or special depreciation allowances. Capital gains taxes are given special consideration.

9. NET PROFIT (after taxes)—Earnings available during the period for distribution or retention.

10. DIVIDENDS—Amount of earnings, if any, distributed to stockholders, if the business is a corporation.

11. RETAINED IN BUSINESS—Net amount that remains from earnings; transferred to earned surplus on the balance sheet. It also reflects, in addition to the depreciations taken, the additional inflow of funds from operations during the period under consideration.

The Monthly P&L—A Working Tool

The monthly profit-and-loss statement, prepared accurately and on time, is perhaps the owner-manager's most valuable working tool. Using the statement to compare performance with the previous month and with the same month a year ago gives him some real guidelines to follow in managing his firm. A condensed monthly report (see figure 7 for sample form) will highlight changes; the owner-manager can then go into his backup accounting records for specifics to use as the basis for further analysis and action. This method not only saves time, it also helps the owner-manager to keep posted on all phases of the enterprise in a systematic manner.

Analysis of percentage changes will indicate areas needing attention; it will help the owner-manager recall transactions and events occurring in the previous month which are factors in the changes. The profit-and-loss statement presents the net effects of such transactions. These might include a sale yielding high or low profits, the sale of old inventory, the payment of bonuses to various employees, the purchase of raw materials at low cost, a new approach in advertising, or an extended period of overtime work in several departments.

Time Needed

The owner-manager needs to decide how much time he can afford to spend on accounting and control information. He should discipline himself and his staff or his accountants to set up the system and develop the figures on time each month; and, even more important, he should *use* the data to improve his performance as a manager. The ever-present tendency among owner-managers is not to run the business, but to let matters go along until a problem develops. Then there is little time to analyze; action is demanded; and a hasty decision often leads to the wrong action.

Cash Flow Projections

Every manager of a small business faces the problem of meeting his payroll or of, often pressing, trade payables. Usually, he will take a piece of paper and list all possible sources of funds as he tries to work his way out of the problem. But why should the manager wait until the last minute to learn of his pressing cash needs? Wouldn't he be better off to have a clear understanding of them in advance?

Using a simple cash flow or cash budgeting technique, a bookkeeper, once trained in a system, can provide monthly data on expected cash requirements and cash resources. With

Figure 7—Form for Monthly Profit and Loss Statement

	This Month	Percent To Sales	Same Month Last Year	Percent To Sales
GROSS SALES				
Discounts and Allowances				
1. NET SALES				
2. COST OF GOODS SOLD				
Direct Material Used				
Direct Labor				
Shop Overhead				
3. GROSS PROFIT				
4. OTHER OPERATING EXPENSES				
Sales Expenses				
Administrative Expenses				
General Expenses				
5. OPERATING PROFIT				
6. Interest and Other Deductions				
7. PROFIT BEFORE TAXES				

COMMENTS

such a program, and using his experience and his ability to forecast coming business, the owner-manager can establish cash flow projections for 6 months or more. Any cash budget is based upon certain assumptions about the following: sales volume, cash sales, payment patterns of accounts receivable, owner's personal withdrawals, and the other elements involved in a cash flow. These assumptions must be realistic, and the owner-manager must understand their relation to overall cash flow. Then he may need to force certain transactions, or perhaps let up on others during certain periods. When major, unexpected events occur, their effect on cash should be quickly determined.

Typical assumptions might be as follows:

1. Sales in a given month will result in 40 percent cash and 60 percent on open book credit.
2. Forty percent of the 60 percent on open book credit will be collected in cash the following month, and the remaining 20 percent will come in a month later.
3. The gross profit margin on sales is 30 percent, and the purchase for inventory will be 50 percent of the following month's anticipated shipments.
4. All inventory purchases are paid in cash during the month in which they are made, and the discounts of from 1 to 2 percent should be taken.
5. A minimum cash balance should be equal to 2 weeks' payroll; and borrowing must be planned on the basis of 3 months' requirements, at which time a forecast of payback must be established.
6. Additional expenses associated with operations and paid during each month are as follows:

Salaries and wages	$2,700
Rent	500
General expenses	750

Cash Forecast Form

If the owner and his bookkeeper realize the use and application of a cash flow, they can make certain they have the data necessary to make better decisions concerning cash. Figure 8 shows a typical cash forecast form; using it, the bookkeeper can keep the owner-manager informed of the daily and weekly progress of cash receipts. And with this information, the manager can advise the bookkeeper on the firm's cash disbursement. It is particularly important that the bookkeeper know trade payable priorities during periods of tight cash. Another very useful tool is the statement of sources and application of funds. Its basic purpose is to show where cash came from and where it was used. It is a counterpart to the cash budget. Both are on a cash basis. The cash budget forecasts the future; the statement of sources and application of funds records the past.

The owner-manager can also use cash flow statements to backstop loan requests. The first questions a loan officer will ask are, "Why do you need the money?" and "How did you determine the amount you need?" Here the information from the cash flow statement provides the answer. The loan officer will then ask, "What did you do with the money your firm had?" The sources and applications statement answers this question.

Semiannually and annually, or during periods of special needs, the accountant should prepare a statement of the firm's sources and applications of funds. From the results, the owner-manager will determine the effective use of equity capital invested and of bank borrowings.

Determining the Break-Even Point

Some owner-managers of small firms may find formal break-even point analysis of little value. If there is frequent change in product mix, profit mix, and volume of business, a formal approach has little value. Small firms rarely have a constant sales unit or product mixture. Sales generally consist of many different job-lots, product lines, or types of services. And they almost always reflect different production or operational costs. The shop or warehouse will probably be processing many different types of orders at any one time. In addition, the work force in the office or shop will vary only slightly, if at all, from week to week. Except for seasonal rushes, when additional full-time and part-time people are needed, normal increases in workload are absorbed by overtime and (perhaps) by people working harder.

The unique set of conditions in small firms is quite different from that in large production shops, where long runs of similar items are common. In general, in smaller firms the amount of variable production, selling, and administrative expenses is small in relation to fixed expenses. This will be true except during a period of major expansion, or when a large amount of the work has to be subcontracted because of the overload of work or because of the special skills required.

In a small manufacturing firm, determination of a break-even point calls for reviewing the previous month's and year's operating experience to determine the ratios of direct labor to sales and direct materials to sales. These ratios will reflect the experienced averages based upon the existing product mix and level of selling prices in the trade. It is then necessary to determine the shop, sales, administrative, and general overhead.

Figure 8—Cash Forecast Form

	January		February		March		April	
	Est.	Act.	Est.	Act.	Est.	Act.	Est.	Act.
Cash balance beginning of month	____	____	____	____	____	____	____	____
RECEIPTS:	____	____	____	____	____	____	____	____
Accounts receivable collections	____	____	____	____	____	____	____	____
Bank loan proceeds	____	____	____	____	____	____	____	____
TOTAL CASH AVAILABLE	____	____	____	____	____	____	____	____
DISBURSEMENTS:								
Trade payables	____	____	____	____	____	____	____	____
Payroll—hourly	____	____	____	____	____	____	____	____
Payroll—salary	____	____	____	____	____	____	____	____
General Expenses	____	____	____	____	____	____	____	____
Selling Expenses	____	____	____	____	____	____	____	____
Capital additions	____	____	____	____	____	____	____	____
Income taxes, local, State, Federal	____	____	____	____	____	____	____	____
Bank loan repayment	____	____	____	____	____	____	____	____
Total disbursements	____	____	____	____	____	____	____	____
CASH BALANCE END OF MONTH	____	____	____	____	____	____	____	____
Less minimum balances	____	____	____	____	____	____	____	____
ESTIMATED AMOUNT OF CASH AVAILABLE	____	____	____	____	____	____	____	____

For example, in the Washburn Manufacturing Company the operating facts for the previous year are as follows:

Direct labor=20 percent of net sales.

Direct material=40 percent of net sales.

Shop, sales, general, and administrative overhead=$156,000 ($3,000 on the average per week, or $13,000 per month).

Peak capacity of the shop with current labor, machinery, and space arrangements—based upon one shift with some overtime and a few part-time helpers—equals $50,000 per month, or about $600,000 per year.

The maximum monthly profit that could be expected is based on the assumption that the work produced and shipped had a direct labor and material content of no more than 60 percent of sales. The resulting contribution to overhead would have been 40 percent of $50,000 maximum shipments, or $20,000. The resulting profit would have been $20,000 minus the expected overhead of $13,000 or $7,000.

A review such as this shows the owner-manager the need for keeping the shop busy. Throughout a 12-month period this may be difficult because there will be periods of low sales, especially in a seasonal business. Sometimes, it is possible to get business at lower prices during these slack periods. But what will be the effect of lower prices on the regular-price business? The owner-manager must control the amount of low-price business he can put into the shop. He must have some way to measure the amount of low-price business he can do and still make a profit. And he may determine this by analyzing his yearly business projections.

In the Washburn Manufacturing Company example, the ratio of labor and materials to selling price is 60 percent. If lower selling prices increase this ratio to 70 percent, for example, the volume of business necessary to cover $13,000 of monthly overhead must also increase.

The owner-manager must understand that profit is not generated until overhead is earned. He must try to sell his product or service at the highest price possible. If he cannot maintain his price level in the face of competition, his firm's break-even point will increase as he decreases his average selling price.

The monthly profit-and-loss statement can be used to test decisions on pricing, sales, and expense control against expectations. By doing this for a period of time, the owner-manager will be able to judge how to price so as to achieve a given volume and profit. In certain situations when demand is seasonal, the owner-manager can use low-price business to balance his overhead and keep his losses to a minimum while keeping his organization intact for the more profitable periods of the year. This approach is sound only if the manager has done a sufficient amount of analysis to know the level of sales he can expect over the entire 12-month period. Predetermined estimates of sales, costs, and possible profits are often very helpful.

Getting Short-Term and Long-Term Money

The owner-manager must, at all times, know his current and prospective cash position. His ability to develop sources of funds to take advantage of business opportunities or to get through tight business periods will help him to make more effective business decisions. Using the cash budget, the manager can distinguish between temporary, short-term needs and permanent, long-term requirements, and he can also determine how much aid he may need.

Sources of Short-Term Funds

Sources for short term money needs are either operations or institutions. The firm should keep a sufficient cash balance to:

1. Take advantage of trade discounts;
2. Maintain a good credit rating in the trade;
3. Retain sufficient funds for business opportunities;
4. Be prepared for emergencies; and
5. Anticipate seasonal needs.

Excessive cash is costly; it ties up funds unnecessarily, and it makes an additional cost which reduces the return on a firm's total assets. If an owner-manager finances his current needs from long-term sources, he may have idle cash for long periods of time. Even if he invests excess funds, he is not likely to earn as much from them as he pays for permanent funds. The crux of effective cash management is in *synchronizing,* as much as possible, dollar inflows (cash receipts) with dollar outflows (cash disbursements).

Funds From Operations

Funds generated from operations are perhaps the most important source of working capital. A monthly review of the profit-and-loss statement will indicate whether funds are being produced from profits or are being liquidated by losses. The owner-manager must determine how much "depreciation" is included in his monthly operating figures, because depreciation is an important source of temporary money.

The "cash" developed from the profit-and-loss statement may well be absorbed into accounts receivable, inventories, or additional fixed asset investments. These must be managed in such a way as to improve the firm's cash position.

Accounts receivable are often an important part of the owner's investment. His credit policies directly affect his working capital. Granting credit is very much like making a short-term loan to customers. For many firms, particularly retail and wholesale establishments, trade credit to customers is a necessary part of regular operations. Firms with sufficient financial strength can use liberal trade credit as a selling tool. Policy on terms of sale and collections have an important effect on a firm's cash flow.

In many firms, invested funds are tied up in inventories. A supermarket or a department store often has a large investment in inventory; but service firms such as filling stations, beauty parlors, or laundromats usually have little or no inventory investment. Other factors may include: seasonality of business, length of production cycle, conditions of purchase of raw materials, and the cost involved in purchasing small and large orders. The firm's cash needs for inventory can be reduced if inventory is very closely planned. If the owner is able to operate with tight inventory controls without losing too many sales, he can use the resulting extra capital for other operating purposes.

Trade credit arising from ordinary business transactions can be an important source of funds. Represented as accounts receivable by the seller and as accounts payable by the buyer, trade credit can be considered a loan equivalent to the value of the goods. Yet the buyer should carefully consider the cost of trade credit. If credit terms are net 30 days, an owner-manager who pays cash within 5 days may be overlooking a valuable "free" source of short-term funds. But if terms are "2/10 net 30," the picture changes. For using the money an additional 20 days, the firm forgoes the 2-percent discount; but figured on a yearly basis, this would be 360 divided by 20 times .02, or 36 percent—obviously, a very expensive way to gain funds.

Sometimes, the larger, well-financed supplier firm uses trade credit to provide a means of financing to its small customers. Liberal dating terms, consignment of goods, and extended payment privileges allow the small firm to have the goods, sell as many as possible, and still retain cash for operating purposes.

The owner-manager must seek the most advantageous trade terms. If he fails to pay his trade debt when it comes due, this vital source of funds will quickly dry up. Delinquency in trade credit is commonly reported to central credit agencies such as Dun & Bradstreet and Lyons, and this information is usually circulated whenever another firm asks for a credit report. Banks also look to the credit reporting agencies, as well as to other trade sources, in determining a firm's credit standing.

Funds From Institutions

When cash from operations is insufficient to meet short-term money requirements, the owner-manager can seek funds from commercial banks or finance companies. Banks' primary functions are to hold deposit funds and to make self-liquidating loans to businesses and individuals. In addition, they can provide valuable financial counsel and criticism. The closer the relationship between the businessman and his banker, the more effectively the banker can help him finance operations during unsuccessful as well as successful periods.

In applying for a loan, the owner-manager must be able to show that planned use of the funds is worthwhile and that he can repay the loan on time. The manager should prepare a projection of his cash needs which will show how the funds will be used; he should be able to show how the borrowed funds will increase his firm's profitability; and he should prepare a *cash flow* showing his proposed schedule for repayment. Conservative estimates are best; if figures are forced, the owner-manager may fail to achieve his goals, and thus weaken his future relations with his bank.

The bank's loan committee will review the owner-manager's loan application. It may insist that he have adequate security to assure repayment; or it may grant an unsecured loan if the facts warrant. The loan conditions imposed are of great importance.

An Unsecured Loan

A decision to grant an unsecured loan usually results from a highly favorable evaluation of the firm's four "C's":

Character
Condition
Capital
Credit

Character refers to the owner-manager's reputation in the trade for honesty and to his handling of his firm's assets. The bank must be able to rely on the owner's managerial skills as well as on his personal honesty.

Condition refers to the firm, the industry, and the product. The bank must understand the unique characteristics of an industry and it must understand a firm's competitive position in an industry. The more a bank knows about an industry, the more effectively it can establish financing.

Capital refers to the owner's investment in his firm. The bank can provide funds for a specific business project having a clear-cut repayment program; but it must have sufficient protection for its funds.

Credit refers to the reputation the owner has for meeting his obligations as they become due. It is an important consideration in the bank's review.

A Secured Loan

If the bank decides to make a secured loan, it may require only the signature of the owner-manager or it may require the pledging of the firm's specific assets and other additional safeguards (such as insurance) to assure repayment.

The major forms of collateral are: accounts receivable, inventory, and fixed assets. An operating business normally generates receivables and inventories that can serve as the primary collateral for a loan. Fixed assets usually serve as supplementary collateral.

Financing through accounts receivable involves either the pledge or *sale* of receivables. Pledging is called accounts-receivable discounting. The bank takes title to the receivables in bulk and loans the firm a negotiated percent of their total value. The firm continues to service the accounts, turning over its collections to the bank. Delinquent accounts will reduce the total borrowing base. Accounts receivable financing involves considerable work, so the cost is higher to the bank.

In factoring, the bank or financial institution *buys* the accounts receivable, notifies the account, and collects directly from it.

Factoring is a common type of financing in the apparel, chemicals, and home furnishings industries. The manufacturers do not have their working capital tied up for 30, 60, or 90 days; and upon shipment of the product, cash can be immediately generated. The amount usually will range from 60 to 90 percent, depending on the particular situation.

Borrowing against inventory is another way of getting funds. The amount which the lender is willing to advance depends on the nature of the product and its marketability. He may be willing to advance 50 to 90 percent of the pledged inventory.

In advancing funds against inventory, the trust receipt, is often used. A trust receipt states that the firm holds the goods in trust for the lender. They can be stored in a public warehouse, on the premises of the borrower, or in the warehouse of an independent third party that acts as the control agent for the lender. Daily "ins" and "outs" are the basis for the financing. One problem of such financing is the requirement that a trust receipt for each bag, carton, box, or tank must be issued. Generally, a trust receipt loan is applied only to non-perishable items that are readily marketable.

Accounts receivable and inventory financing are useful for meeting short-term and intermediate-term credit needs. Because they provide security for loans, they increase the ability of firms with low credit ratings to obtain financing. Many small firms use this type of financing while they are growing and getting better established.

Sources of Long-Term Funds

Long-term loans—those for more than a year—are available from the following sources:

1. Installment financing of equipment or machinery.
2. Equipment leasing.
3. Real estate financing.
4. Commercial banks.
5. Insurance companies, pension funds, etc.
6. Local or State development and credit corporations.
7. Small Business Administration lending programs.
8. Small Business Investment Companies (SBIC's).

Installment financing of income-producing equipment or machinery amortizes the debt over a scheduled period. Installment payments are based upon the expected increase in income arising from use of the equipment. The financing agency, which may be the manufacturer, holds title to the equipment, usually in the form of a conditional sales contract that is essentially a chattel mortgage. Other names for conditional sales contracts are "special budget plans" or "easy-payment plans."

Equipment leasing, a relatively new form of financing, can be done in two ways: A firm may arrange for the use of another party's property by paying a rental fee. Or a manufacturing firm which already owns the equipment may sell it and then lease it back for continued use for a given period of time (sale and lease-back).

Real estate financing lessens the drain on cash payback because of the long span of time involved in the mortgage contract. And occasionally, appreciation in the value of real estate enables the owner-manager to refinance the original loan.

Commercial bank financing is a common source of funds for the small firm. Loans are from 1 year to usually not more than 8 years. Bank requirements for long-term loans are more restrictive than for short-term loans. A typical loan agreement may require the borrower to:

1. Maintain a specific minimum of working capital
2. Furnish certified financial statements periodically
3. Other loan conditions considered necessary to assure repayment of the loan.

The agreement commonly contains a statement covering the obligations of the borrower in the event of default. One common feature is an "acceleration clause," under which any breach of agreement by the borrower will cause the entire amount of the debt to become due immediately.

Insurance companies, pension funds, and trust funds have shown an increasing willingness to make loans to small and medium-size firms. Typically, these institutions grant loans for a period of not less than 10 years or more than 20 years. An applicant must meet very rigid financial standards to qualify for a loan from these sources, and an iron-clad agreement is entered into.

Local or State development and credit corporations usually confine their loans to firms whose credit may not be acceptable to commercial banks. They supply long-term funds to small firms which will strengthen the State and/or local economy. For their extended risk, they may receive common stock options or warrants as part of the financing. State laws vary somewhat in this type of financing.

The Small Business Administration has a varied program of financial assistance. Whenever possible, the applicant is directed to available private sources of credit. SBA makes direct loans only after other possibilities for assistance have been exhausted.

It is the policy of SBA to encourage loans to small firms by banks and other private lending institutions. However, if the entire amount of a loan cannot be obtained from such sources, SBA will consider *guaranteeing* a loan or *participating* in the loan with a bank or other lending institution. Generally SBA may guarantee or participate up to 90 percent of the amount of the loan, but the SBA portion to any one borrower cannot legaly exceed $350,000. Under law, SBA cannot enter into an immediate participation agreement if a guaranteed loan is possible.

The maturity of a loan in which SBA participates may not exceed 10 years, except that the portion of a loan for constructing facilities may have a maturity of 15 years. The interest rate on the SBA share is 5½ percent on the bank's share of immediate participation loans, and on guaranteed loans, the interest rate is set by the bank, up to 8 percent. If a businessman's bank is unable to extend needed credit wholly in the form of a bank loan or to make the loan in participation with SBA, then the businessman may apply for the loan directly at an SBA field office.

Small Business Investment Companies (SBIC's) are another source of long-term funds. The Small Business Administration licenses, regulates, and helps finance privately owned SBIC's. They, in turn, fill a gap in small business financing by extending equity capital and long-term loans to small firms. Under the Small Business Investment Act of 1958 and under SBA's regulations, an SBIC may finance a small business:

By purchase of the firm's convertible debentures.

By purchase of capital stock in the firm, with or without purchase warrants to acquire additional stock.

By purchase of debt securities, with or without warrants to purchase stock.

By any other acceptable instrument of equity financing.

By making long-term loans to the firm.

Financing provided by an SBIC must be for a minimum of 5 years, and loans may be granted for as long as 20 years. Shorter-term loans (less than 5 years) may be made when necessary to protect previous investments of an SBIC. Also, loans may be extended for 10 years if this will aid the small business in the orderly liquidation of the loan. If the amount of funds needed is greater than one particular SBIC can provide, it may be possible to get other SBIC's to participate in a loan or to purchase a firm's debentures.

Equity Financing

Original funds and subsequent earnings retained in a business make up its equity capital.

The owner-manager's decision to sell some of his firm's stock to outsiders requires a great deal of consideration and work. He must try to determine long-term advantages and disadvantages for himself, his firm, and his estate. Before making a decision, he should discuss the pros and cons with his accountant, lawyer, banker, investment banker, or financial consultant. Possible buyers of his stock would include:

Employees.

Friends of owner or of employees.

Venture capital groups or organizations.

Small Business Investment Companies.

Institutional investors.

Individuals.

Some of the advantages of raising equity capital are as follows:

The funds raised do not have to be paid back.

There is no fixed annual interest expense.

Raising equity capital can bring additional bank financing and/or reduce the cost of borrowing.

The manager may be able to capitalize on a favorable price/earnings ratio and sell stock for values far greater than the net worth.

Public financing or sale of stock may ultimately increase the principal's net income through the growth of the firm; and it may protect the estate of the principals.

Once the owner-manager sells stock to the public, he is in a position to establish stock options to attract and hold key people.

The most common stumbling block for the owner-manager when considering equity financing is the fear of losing control. Executives of smaller firms who have worked hard to build their enterprise naturally fear giving up any of their precious freedom of action. On the other hand, if well selected, the new stockholders will have genuine interest in the growth of the firm, and the owner-manager will be in a position to benefit from the use of their management skills.

Control of the firm is much more likely to be jeopardized when a large minority interest is sold to one person or to a closed group than when stock is sold widely to the public. The initial cost of broad public financing is likely to be high—much pathbreaking work is required by accountants, lawyers, and so forth.

The specific time when stock may be sold to the public is, in the final analysis, determined by the investment banking community. The degree of public interest will depend upon the overall securities market, the size of the issue, general business conditions, and the past, present, and expected performance of the firm. The following situations are representative of those which build interest in the public market:

A product or service has proved successful locally and shows the potential to succeed regionally or nationally.

A new product has become so successful that an allied new line is in demand.

An old-line, conservative firm needs to broaden its line so as to lower unit distribution and marketing costs.

A new applied-science product requires additional funds to manufacture and sell or to continue research and development.

Already proved profitable, a new merchandising scheme requires added funds.

Several small, independent firms wish to merge, forming one large company with a new corporate image.

There is a need to purchase new equipment or to add working capital—both being used as a base for future expansion.

Equity capital provides increased financial strength to the firm because it is the basis for obtaining other forms of financing. The owner-manager must consider the long-range effects of equity financing on his firm and the net effects on his personal position. If his firm is growing and if the addition of equity funds would allow even faster growth, then the owner-manager's personal estate will probably be greatly improved too.

The Importance of Financial Planning and Control

The successful small business man faces continuous change as his firm grows and his profits increase. With these changes, he is exposed to unknowns which can have an ultimately bad effect on the firm's finances. Effective response to change depends upon understanding and using financial planning as well as upon good luck. The attitude of "I've been successful up to now, so who needs financial planning?" can lead any firm into deep trouble.

Financial Planning

Basically, the aims and purposes of financial planning are:

To achieve a fair return on invested capital (net worth).

To maintain satisfactory working capital.

To maintain a proper balance among accounts receivable, inventory, and fixed assets.

To evaluate the effects of markets, products, competition, and sales levels upon gross profits.

To relate the firm's overhead to its gross profits.

To maintain satisfactory capitalization.

To anticipate problems that would arise if the owner-manager were to die.

The owner-managers of most small firms fail to give adequate consideration to their financial affairs until a severe problem develops. Typically, the owner is unwilling to invest the necessary time, or he doesn't understand the overall financial aspects of his business. Yet, in many instances, particularly in *very* small firms, the amount of time required for proper financial planning may be as little as one evening a month.

To formulate a simple, workable financial plan, the owner-manager, with the aid of any advisers he may have, must develop and use the financial tools discussed earlier. He must demand monthly or quarterly profit-and-loss figures and balance sheets. These reports should be kept on file for at least 5 years, so that the manager can review the firm's prior performance record. As the reports are reviewed, the manager should make notes which explain the firm's good or bad performance. He should keep these notes with the reports so that he can readily recall the reasons for the results obtained. If the firm is very small, the cost of preparing these statistics shouldn't be too high. The cost of acquiring necessary accounting data on past performance is indeed a very small price to pay for the insurance afforded by having it.

Once the accounting information is generated and maintained for a period, the owner-manager and his advisers will have a base upon which to develop a financial plan. They can then determine the financial effects on the profit-and-loss statement, balance sheet, and cash flow of such items as increasing sales, introduction of new products, new promotional expenses and advertising, new equipment, real estate transactions, new credit policy, a new pricing program, a new inventory program, and so forth. It is not very difficult to develop rough financial figures which can show the effects of new ideas upon the firm's future operating statement, balance sheet, and cash flow. Even rough figures can quickly indicate the firm's possible gain or loss and the resulting financial problems, if any, that will develop.

The owner-manager should develop a financial plan which will indicate the level of sales and gross profits at which he can add overhead, and the levels at which he must reduce expenses. Instead of driving blindly ahead in uncertainty about the firm's success, he will know more clearly what strategy to follow to keep the firm operating effectively—even if this means adding staff (at the proper time).

What may happen without a financial plan is illustrated in the case of Bruce Electronic Distributors, Inc. For several years, Bruce King, the owner, kept up a very hectic pace; he directly supervised his outside salesforce, his inside salesforce, his warehouse operation, and his office. Everyone Bruce hired geared himself to working long hours to follow the pattern he had established. The firm made money every year; from a very small investment, Bruce had built up a net worth of around $400,000. For the past 2 years, Bruce took out a nominal salary of $12,000, and aftertax earnings were only $13,000, and $9,500. Bruce found himself running short of cash.

Bruce eventually discussed his problem with his accountant and his banker. Both these men said that while they were not in close touch with the business, because Bruce never conferred with either of them, the business appeared to have a number of real financial problems. In spite of past success, the firm seemed to be floundering along on an uncharted course.

The banker and accountant agreed on the following:

Bruce had received a very low return on his investment during the preceding 4 years.

Inventory was too high; many lines were overstocked and/or obsolete.

Accounts receivable were stretched out with too many delinquent accounts "over 90 days."

The new building was costly, being too big and poorly located.

Although operating expenses were low, gross profit had continued to drop in the last 4 years; and certain product lines showed very poor gross profits.

Earned purchase discounts were too low because King didn't borrow the necessary funds (which were easily available), nor did he direct his bookkeeper to take all trade discounts.

In effect, Bruce King had failed to manage the financial affairs of his firm properly. Although he kept overhead low, gross profits in the past 4 years had been forced down because of increasing competition and the failure to develop a new merchandising strategy. With the aid of his advisers, Bruce devised a plan which called for hiring a sales manager to direct inside and outside sales. Thus he was released to seek new lines to distribute, to reduce the current inventory, and to collect the accounts receivable more promptly.

Bruce King paid a high price for his failure to develop a financial plan; namely, he got increasingly poor return on his investment. The personal aggravation he suffered could have been reduced if he had analyzed his situation and taken the proper steps to improve it.

Using A Financial Forecast and Budget

Making up a financial forecast and budget may seem unnecessary to an owner-manager. Yet, they are excellent tools to make him think carefully about the future directions in which his company might move.

Developing a simple financial forecast and budget involves thinking through a course of action and making an organized analysis of its ramifications. Essentially, forecasting deals with the effects of outside forces upon the sales of the firm, and what this implies for the firm's resource requirements. Budgeting takes a forecast of sales and of resource needs and traces their effects upon production, purchasing, material schedules, the profit-and-loss statement, the balance sheet, and the cash flows. Taken together, the financial forecast and the financial budget show the actual timing of major financial events and will bring to light the leads and lags that are at the heart of financial planning. (See figure 8 for a sample form.)

The forecast and budget are useful not only as a basis for planning, but also as a basis for controlling operations. By expressing the company's plans in financial form, the budget forces the owner-manager to look ahead. This means that he is in a position to identify and study problems before they blow up in front of him. When developing a budget, the owner-manager must review the firm's previous performance, for it is upon this that he will base his future objectives. Such a review tells the owner-manager more about his firm's financial activities; and with this added information, he can more effectively delegate authority to subordinates without loss of control.

The owner-manager can tie in his financial forecast and budget to his system of day-to-day operating controls. For example, in a machine shop, the weekly ratio of direct labor to sales should be roughly equal to the forecasted monthly ratio of direct labor to sales. The weekly ratio is determined from what may be called "cuff controls." That is, sales will be obtained from shipments billed and direct labor will be determined from the weekly payroll. In many small firms, the weekly billing may vary between the first, second, third, and fourth week of each month. Sometimes, instead of equal weekly shipments of 25 percent of the month's goal, it may actually be 15 percent the first week, 20 percent the second week, 30 percent the third week, and 35 percent in the fourth week. Adjustment of the weekly ratio to the peculiarities of shipping practices will then reflect their true weekly movement toward the established monthly forecast. Should problems develop, the owner-manager can make corrections *during the month,* before it is too late. In summary, budget forces the manager to reflect on:

Projected sales.
Needed production levels.
Materials and purchasing requirements.
Expected direct labor needs.
Allowable expenses.
Forecasted effects on P & L statement, balance sheet, and cash flow.

The Owner-Manager's Personal Skills

The amount of time an owner-manager must devote to marketing, operations, and finance will vary with the type and size of firm and its financial strength. Usually, an owner-manager will tend to spend his time in those phases of the business with which he is most familiar. Generally, owner-managers have more knowhow in marketing and production than in finances. By concentrating their efforts where they have knowhow, they often *remain* relatively ignorant of the financial aspects of their businesses.

Assessing the Owner-Manager's Skills

The owner-manager must assess his personal skills in finances. He must understand the financial tools needed for the successful operation of his firm and make the necessary arrangements for their preparation and use. If he is unable personally to perpare the required financial planning and control data, he should acquire the assistance of a bookkeeper, comptroller, or accountant.

Once the data are prepared, he must review the figures to know what is going on in his business and to be able to interpret the information so that he can make more effective decisions. He must be able to recognize weaknesses in his financial reporting system as his firm grows or otherwise changes. He should know which types of data he should be receiving daily, weekly, monthly, and quarterly. He must continuously check the accuracy of the information he receives.

The accounting and financial reporting program of the firm, if it is to be of value to the owner-manager, must be prepared on time. This can only be accomplished through continuous discipline. The firm may have on its staff a bookkeeper, office manager, or comptroller who is well disciplined and can see to it that the financial information is prepared accurately and on time; but the owner-manager is responsible for knowing how good or how poor a job is being done in his firm at all times.

The firm's accountant can assist the owner-manager in the firm's internal financial management activities. He can help the owner-manager learn how to interpret the balance sheet, profit-and-loss statement, and cash projection; and he can assist in preparing financial forecasts and budgets.

Under no reasonable circumstances should an outside accountant prepare financial information that the owner-manager does not understand. To be unable to interpret the condition of his business most often would lead a manager to make poor decisions.

Dick Sessions was forced into expanding the activities of Sessions Hardware Company from a wholesale distributorship into a retail business. This happened when his biggest customer, who owned two retail units, notified Dick, his major creditor, that he was planning to go into bankruptcy. Dick, with the advice and counsel of his attorney, took control of the two units and made the necessary arrangements with the other creditors. Placing the retail units under the direction of his brother-in-law, Dick worked very hard to clean up the stores' inventories and to increase sales. At the end of the first year of operations, the firm's cash position was very poor, but the accountant's profit-and-loss statement showed that they had made money. Dick was at a loss to know where the profit had been earned and what had happened to the cash account—until he got his accountant to give him separate figures for the wholesale and retail operations.

Plans were made to develop over the following year a financial forecast and budget as well as a cash projection for 3 months at a time. Each month, the figures were to be reviewed by the accountant and Dick. At that time, they discussed the forecast for the next 3-month period and made the necessary adjustments to the original estimates.

Dick committed an error very common among small business owner-managers. He failed to foresee his financial information needs under the new setup. Because of the cash bind, he was forced to ask questions. If this problem had not developed, the accountant might well have continued reporting Sessions Company operating figures on a consolidated basis, and Dick would have continued to be in the dark on how well his distribution business and retail hardware business compared in performance.

Dick had no specific data on the month-to-month success or failure of his expanded enterprise. To be sure, he knew his firm was profitable; but by use of a simple financial forecast and budget for each of his divisions, he would probably have been able to observe changes in the gross profits in each of his operations. His use of a cash projection could very well have enabled him to reduce his inventory or purchases or perhaps to concentrate his efforts more effectively on the firm's accounts receivables.

Dick's success over the years had brought very few financial problems. He hadn't been forced to improve his skills in financial management. He had directed his energies to other phases of the business; and, as a result, he was ill equipped to deal with the new situation.

Developing a Staff

It is the responsibility of the owner-manager to recognize the needs of his firm in the area of financial planning and control. Even if a firm is very small, the owner-manager's personal efforts can be deployed more effectively through proper use of the financial information developed. The smaller the firm, the fewer the number of key subordinates employed, and hence the faster the necessary financial data can be generated.

In a small but growing firm, various skills, in financial management will be needed at successive stages of growth:

A 1-to-10-employee firm may use a part-time bookkeeper or accountant.

A 10-to-20-employee business may employ a full-time bookkeeper and the regular services of an accountant.

A 20-to-50 employee firm may use the services of a bookkeeper or of an office manager-bookkeeper combination and the regular services of a public accounting firm.

A 50-to-200-employee firm may require the services of a comptroller who would work with the firm's auditors.

With more than 200 employees, the firm may establish, in addition to a comptroller, the position of treasurer.

The owner-manager must decide at which point in the growth of his firm additional skills are required. The exact timing will depend on his own skills in financial management and the degree of interest he may have for performing this function himself at that particular time.

If the owner-manager has little or no background and experience in accounting and financial management, he must try to get the services of the most qualified bookkeeper available. He should also seek the services of an accounting firm which will help him improve his knowledge of this phase of the business. Seeking the right firm, he should talk with other businessmen, his suppliers, his banker, and others. And he should talk to more than one accounting firm so that he can become familiar with the varied types of services offered.

Calling upon Outsiders for Help

The business community has many trained persons who can help the owner-manager direct the financial management activities of his firm. Available to work with the firm's systems and records on a part-time basis would be bookkeepers, accountants, business recordkeeping firms, management consultants, stockholders, and some trade associations. Professional help would include accountants, lawyers, bankers, investment bankers, suppliers, credit managers, large customers, financial consultants, various government agencies (including the Financial Assistance Division of the Small Business Administration), and educational institutions.

Summary

As the financial manager of his firm, it is the owner-manager's responsibility to make the most effective use of the invested capital. He must use the tools of financial management to guide the firm's resources into the most profitable lines and to keep a tight control on costs. To be successful, he must understand and use such financial tools as the balance sheet, ratio analysis, profit-and-loss statement, cash flow, source and application of funds, and break-even point.

The time he invests in developing his personal skills in financial planning and control will yield greater profits. He will be more knowledgeable about the firm's cash needs and about accounts receivable and inventories. Ability to understand the importance of proper inventory-taking and evaluation as a basis for determining an accurate profit picture is vital. In addition, the owner-manager must recognize the effects of a conservative inventory policy on net worth, particularly when he considers the firm's "true" return on investment.

The importance of developing and using profit-and-loss statements which accurately reflect the performance of the firm cannot be overstated. The operating statement is a vital tool for measuring the effectiveness of the firm. Monthly P&L statements are most desirable, but they may not always be feasible.

Using ratio analysis on his balance sheet and P&L statement will help the owner-manager to note quickly those areas of potential weakness. His further use of these ratios in comparing his firm's performance with others in his trade and other firms of similar size in different fields will also be of real value. Recognition that members of the financial community use ratio analysis to evaluate firms should further stimulate interest in using this tool.

Simple cash flow projections and statements of sources and application of funds will highlight for the manager what has happened, what is happening, and what is going to happen to his cash needs. Early recognition of his money needs will enable the owner-manager to be more effective in raising both short-term and long-term capital. A rough 12-month cash projection, perhaps developed with the assistance of the firm's accountant, will give the owner-manager a good idea of the range of his cash needs.

Because of the rapid changes in product mix, product profit mixture, and sales levels, the use of a formal break-even chart in most small firms is impractical. However, the owner-manager, with the aid of his accountant, can rather accurately determine the firm's relatively fixed overhead for a given volume of sales. Further analysis of the expected gross profit percentage, from the type of business being handled during a given period, can then be used to determine the approximate sales level required for a break-even performance. This approach requires the owner-manager to be always aware of the gross profit of respective lines. He will quickly recognize the importance of doing business during slack periods if only to contribute to the reduction of overhead.

Success in getting a higher return on the investment in his firm can frequently be accelerated by the owner-manager's improving his knowhow as a financial manager. He doesn't require the depth of accounting knowledge possessed by his accountant, but he does need a general understanding of the application of the tools of financial management. He should recognize that although sales and shipments result from the time and skills he directs toward sales and operations, he must also devote some time to improving his skills in finance so that he can guide his firm more effectively to the profit goals desired.

Chapter 5

CREDIT AND COLLECTIONS

CREDIT and collection affect every small business in the purchase or sale of goods or services. Credit to customers can help build a firm in many ways; yet a liberal credit policy contains risks that must be considered. The importance of collection activities may vary, but they must always be managed so that the firm maintains sufficient working capital.

The owner-manager of a small business must train himself in credit and collection management, and he must understand their effect on his current and long-range business interests.

Value of Credit to the Small Firm

The owner of a small firm, whether retail, wholesale, manufacturing, or service, must understand the use of credit in his business, and he must learn how to handle it. About 90 percent of all sales by manufacturers and wholesalers and 40 percent of those by retailers are on credit. Because so much of the small firm's capital is apt to be tied up in accounts receivable, credit management is particularly important to it.

Likewise, credit policies of suppliers are a vital factor. If firms have enough cash, they can take advantage of special purchases of such things as seasonal overruns and overstocks, or they can profit from special deals such as auctions or factory closings.

Credit and the Small Firm

Consumer credit is extended by a retailer to his customers —a large group whose purchases may occur over an extended interval. *Business credit* is extended by manufacturers and wholesalers to their customers, which are other business firms.

The following aspects of credit are important to the businessman:

1. Credit terms.
2. To whom credit will be extended.
3. Maximum credit limits.
4. Use of credit insurance.
5. Records needed.
6. Collection program.

Credit is time allowed for payment for goods and services already delivered to the customer. Credit implies trust that the payment will be made. The element of risk in credit is that the customer will not pay, or else will pay late and tie up the seller's funds unprofitably. Most business credit is on an "open account" (for other kinds of terms, see figure 9). Common types of consumer credit are open accounts or charge accounts, installment accounts, budget accounts, and revolving credit accounts.

The terms of sale extended by a small firm have significant effects on its cash needs. Special incentives offered to customers for early payment can be *very expensive;* in many instances, it may be wiser to offer normal trade terms and borrow funds that may be needed.

An example of this is the experience of the Williams Machine Company. Jack Williams, the owner, found that in July and August of last year he was pressed for funds. So he offered his major customers an additional 2 percent discount during those months. When Jack changed accountants, the new accountant questioned this practice. After considerable discussion, a cash flow projection was developed for the critical 2-month period. The new accountant also showed Jack that it was cheaper to use short-term bank loans than to offer his customers additional discounts. Jack's banker welcomed the opportunity to provide the necessary loans.

Figure 9—Common Business Credit Sales Terms

Term	Explanation
3/10, 1/15, n/60	3 percent discount for first 10 days; 1 percent discount for 15 days; bill due net on 60th day.
M.O.M. (Middle of month)	Billing will be on the 15th of the month (middle of the month), including all purchases made since the middle of the previous month.
E.O.M. (End of month)	Billing at end of month, covering all credit purchases of that month.
C.W.O. or C.I.A. (Cash with order, or Cash in advance)	Orders received are not processed until advanced payment is received.
C.B.D. (Cash before delivery)	Merchandise may be prepared and packaged by the seller, but shipment is not made until payment is received.
C.O.D. (Cash on delivery)	Amount of bill will be collected upon delivery of goods.
S.D. — B.L. (Sight draft—Bill of lading)	A negotiable bill of lading, accompanied by the invoice and a sight draft drawn on the buyer, is forwarded by the seller to the customer's bank. The bill of lading is released by the bank to the customer only upon his honoring the draft.
2/10, n/30, *R.O.G. (Receipt of goods)	2 percent discount for 10 days; bill due net on 30th day—but both discount period and 30 days start from the date of receipt of the goods, not from the date of the sale.
2/10, n/30, M.O.M.	2 percent discount for 10 days; bill due net on 30th day—but both periods start from the 15th of the month following the sales date.
2/10, n/30, E.O.M.	2 percent discount for 10 days; bill due net on 30th day—but both periods start from the end of the month in which the sale was made.
8/10, E.O.M.	8 percent discount for 10 days; bill due net on 30th day—but both periods start from the end of the month following the sales date.

Sales date is the day that the shipment was made. It will generally be the same date shown on the invoice. In consumer credit, the sales date is the day the sale was made and may or may not coincide with the date of shipment.

***The owner-manager should keep in mind that 2%/10, n/30 amounts to 36.5 percent in annual interest calculation:**

$$\frac{2\%}{30 - 10} \times 365 = 36.5\%$$

Using Credit to Increase Sales

The owner-manager must decide how much credit he will offer. The value of credit as a sales tool will depend on the type of business, the credit policy of competitors, the buying habits of customers, and the amount of working capital available. Also, its advantages must outweigh its costs.

The chief advantages of a credit program are that charge or special credit customers are more likely to be regular purchasers than are those who pay cash; and charge customers can be better satisfied by exchanges and adjustments, thus helping the close relationship.

In many areas of retailing, credit-granting firms are more profitable and do a larger volume of business than "strictly cash" stores, even though the prices of the credit stores are slightly higher. The long-run trend seems to be an increase in credit activity—particularly in very competitive situations.

Certain manufacturing and wholesaling fields develop unique credit arrangements so that they can effectively produce and distribute their goods even in the slack season. The intent is to get their products to the point of sale as early as possible so that the retailer can have sufficient seasonal inventories. This also allows for early reorder of fast-moving lines. The manufacturer and distributor benefit additionally by keeping their warehouse inventories low and available for the buildup of additional backup stocks. The favorable credit terms offered help in "forcing the distribution" of many products. The old saying "You can't do business off an empty wagon" is avoided by using a creative credit approach in building sales.

Pitfalls in Credit and Collection Management

Poor credit and collection management can jeopardize an otherwise efficient firm. Failure to evaluate the credit standing of new customers and allowing old accounts to overextend their credit are two examples of ineffective credit and collection management.

Effects on Working Capital

Granting extensive credit is likely to cause a real strain on the thinly capitalized small firm. As sales build up, accounts receivable tend to increase proportionally. And if the allowed time for payment is extended, the amount of capital tied up will rise even more. The rate of increase will vary with the type of business. A typical retailer will have $65—his cost of goods—in a sales increase of $100. (Of course, various items of overhead and expense must also be met; all salaries must be paid each week.) For the manufacturer, a $100 increase in sales requires an extra $75 in cash to meet direct costs. The wholesaler's cash needs are even heavier—$85 for every $100 increase in sales.

In recognizing how increased sales will affect his working capital, the owner-manager must plan accordingly. He should look to his suppliers for some support during periods of expanding sales, particularly when the increased sales result from conservative credit extension policy. Suppliers will fre quently grant special dating terms, or they will accept promissory notes or trade acceptances. Sometimes, consigned goods with special credit arrangements will be offiered.

Some lines of business—such as bakery products, grocery products, and milk—call for quick payment of accounts receivable. Others—such as construction, machinery, office equipment, etc.,—usually offer longer terms.

A sale is really not a sale until the invoice is paid in full. In trying to develop additional sales, the owner-manager frequently overlooks the amount of debts owed the firm. All too often, small businesses fail because the job of collection is poorly done. In some cases, there is *no* collection activity at all!

If he is personally not interested in collecting accounts receivable, the owner-manager *must* assign the responsiblity to someone in his organization. In very small firms, the bookkeeper usually gets the job. Busy with the bookkeeping functions, however, he rarely has the necessary time to devote to collections. Therefore, it should be someone else.

Credit and Collection Problems

If credit and collection are left to take care of themselves, the firm and its owner will face many problems which have, in effect, been self-created. Areas for concern include the following:

1. Slow-paying customers.
2. Bad debt losses which must be written off.
3. Over-extended credit, beyond firm's financial capacity, resulting in insufficient working capital.
4. Failure to evaluate credit standing of new customers.
5. Added costs of borrowing because of too liberal credit policy.
6. Credit customers' excessive use of the returned goods privilege.
7. Operating and overhead costs of the credit and collection activities; these include the expenses of credit investigation, billing, and collection.

8. Destruction of a good credit and collection program through the intrusion of personal relationships, a common happening in small firms.

To forestall such problems, the owner-manager must be prepared for them. Some manufacturers and wholesalers use credit insurance to protect themselves from "abnormal" bad debt losses resulting from natural disasters, poor industry conditions, a business recession, or other unexpected conditions. (The insurance firm calculates the "normal" loss rate on the basis of industry experience and the loss record of the particular firm.)

Credit insurance is available only to manufacturers and wholesalers that sell to other business firms. There are two reasons for this: First, it is difficult to analyze the risk involved in selling to ultimate consumers. Second, retailers' need for credit insurance is less acute because their risk is usually spread among a greater number of customers. In some situations, it may be desirable to have credit insurance on specific business accounts rather than general coverage. Higher percentages of coinsurance are required for inferior accounts in order to discourage reckless credit extension by insured firms. Accounts are classified according to ratings by Dun & Bradstreet or other recognized agencies. Premiums vary with account ratings.

The retailer's cost of extending credit may be offset by the interest or carrying charge. Yet even with what appears to be an adequate rate, the firm must be very careful in calculating the true cost of its credit and collection activities. Costs include not only handling credit applications, but also making credit analyses, establishing accounts receivable ledger cards, receiving payments, sending out statements, and dunning overdue accounts. Bad debt losses can develop even after the best effort And unsound decisions in credit and collection management can be one of the steps that lead to bankruptcy.

Keeping Accurate Credit and Collection Data

The owner-manager of a small firm must know what kinds of information are needed to operate an effective credit program. As a firm grows, more elaborate forms and records will be required. Knowing *when* particular forms should be added is the responsibility of the manager. Proper timing depends upon the rate of growth of the firm, the relative amount of capital tied up in the accounts receivable, and the amount of credit risk involved in the firm's particular trade.

The purpose in adding forms and records as the firm grows is to reduce the burden on the memory of the manager and, as a result, reduce the chances of mistakes. The owner can rely on up-to-date and accurately written credit data. The easy and quick availability of facts will allow him to make more effective credit decisions.

Records Needed

The types of forms and records commonly used for consumer and business credit include:

Credit application form.
Credit reports from outside agencies.
Customer credit file.
Collateral forms.
Accounts receivable ledger cards.
Invoices.
Statements.
Monthly list of aged accounts receivables.
Tickler file or other followup system.
Collection letters.

Companies that make and/or sell paper forms or one of the credit or financial agencies in the community can help the owner-manager design the forms best suited for his own needs. At the beginning of a credit program, it is important that the owner be interested and involved in the development of the forms and records so that he will know what is going on and be able to lend his experience to setting up the proper records. And as a practical matter, if the owner-manager knows the reasons for and the values of the new records, he will be more apt to support their maintenance.

Systems and Procedures

When the manager withdraws from active guidance of the credit program (as a result of increased demands on his time from other managerial duties), he must have established systems and procedures that others can follow to assure effective credit and collection management. The members of his organization should be able to answer, in a routine manner, such questions as:

What is this customer's proper credit limit?
Are the credit terms correct?
Should this customer be shipped C.O.D. or open line?
Should the customer be asked to supply some collateral?
Should credit insurance be used for this account?
How much pressure should be exerted in collecting from a specific account at a particular time?
Should this account be turned over to a lawyer for collection?

The answers to these questions can, in large part, be determined from the firm's previous experience with accounts. The handling of day-to-day credit and collection problems should be systematic, so that comparable events will be handled similarly. Routine matters can be processed according to established policies, but nonroutine or special situations should be brought to the attention of the owner-manager quickly.

Jack Woolson, owner of Woolson Filling Stations, developed a serious credit problem. Enlarging his stations from two to six in a 3-month period, he personally hired all employees and trained them in the handling of credit. But within another 3 months, he found a very large number of old accounts receivable that were uncollectable. It took Jack's bookkeeper more than 2 months more to determine that two of the new station attendants, who worked evenings only, were extending credit to customers unauthorized to receive it. They had, in fact, given credit to a number of customers on the firm's list of poor credit risks. The firm's procedure and system called for having credit sales checked at the home office every day. But because of the overload of work in the office, this important procedure had been bypassed and the resulting losses had occurred.

Woolson Filling Stations' losses could have been avoided had Jack maintained the original systems and procedures that worked so successfully. His lack of planning and poor credit discipline proved to be very costly, and they would have been avoidable if precautions had been taken in time.

Sources of Credit Information

The manager of a small firm should get to know and understand the various sources of credit information. Certain types of information are sold by the mercantile credit agencies; other types are available from them as a service or on an exchange-of-information basis.

Arrangements can be made with suppliers' credit departments to exchange information. This type of interchange can be very valuable when up-to-date sales and payment records of current or prospective customers are being sought. The owner-manager should recognize that his firm's performance with major suppliers is also a matter of record in his trade.

Banks can be very helpful information sources about their depositors. Often, they can give excellent advice on the amount of credit a depositor can handle. They can also help get credit information on out-of-town customers—particularly if speed is important to process a new order or to check out a possible bankruptcy situation. The owner-manager should be careful not to take advantage of his banker by making too many requests for credit information.

Firms needing daily credit information—for example, a retailer checking on consumer credit applications—should consider buying the services of local credit bureaus. They are particularly effective in rating persons living in the local trading area; and their effectiveness is extended through their cooperation with the International Consumer Credit Association (formerly the National Retail Credit Association) or the Associated Credit Bureaus of America. These associations develop credit information on persons who have moved from one town to another.

Services offered by credit bureaus include: Checks on newcomers in the trading area; written and telephone credit information on individuals; data on changes in customers' credit risk status; assistance on tracing customers who leave town without providing a forwarding address; and collection of poor risks accounts.

A typical consumer credit report would include such information as: Credit accounts maintained, history of purchases, balances due, promptness of payment, and period that the account is maintained; consumer's net worth (home, car, etc); employment verification (data on income, position, and duration of job); and character information and police record, if any.

A firm need not be a member of the local bureau to obtain credit information; usually, however, the nonmember firm pays higher charges for the services.

Manufacturers and wholesalers often use the services of *mercantile* credit agencies. Privately owned and operated, these agencies continuously collect, analyze, and evaluate credit information on business firms. Their credit ratings are based upon the observed experience of the reporting firms. Services are by fee, based on the range required.

Among the general mercantile agencies, Dun & Bradstreet, covering many fields throughout the country, is the best known. D & B offers its reference book, credit reports, and other special information to firms that buy its service. The reference book includes credit ratings, evaluations of financial strength, and other vital credit information. Lyon Furniture Merchantile Agency provides data on furniture retailers for furniture manufacturers and wholesalers. The Jewelers Board of Trade offers similar services to the jewelry industry. The National Credit Office, originally organized to handle credit inquiries in the principal textile trades, now also reports on banking, metals, electronics, leather, furniture, paint, rubber, and chemicals.

If the owner-manager uses the services of a factor, he can avoid maintaining a credit and collection system. The factor establishes a working procedure for clearing credit for new customers; setting up credit limits for old customers; and for collecting accounts receivable. He then *buys* accounts receivable outright from the selling firm.

The owner-manager should also keep in touch with competitors and other firms whose activities are related to his customers. The exchange of credit information between businessmen can be quite valuable—particularly if a customer's financial position weakens. Timing is vital if the owner-manager hopes to protect his position as a creditor.

Sources of Credit and Collection Management Assistance

Good credit and collection management can help prevent serious losses of capital and can aid more effective use of invested funds. If the owner-manager does not have the proper abilities, he must either improve himself or pay for the services of professionals. One means of self-improvement is working closely with one or more of the following (in addition to the firm's accountant and lawyer):

Suppliers' credit managers.
Local credit agency staff.
Bankers.
Other businessmen.
Factors.
Trade association staff.
Financial consultants.

For example, the credit executive of a firm's major supplier can be of real practical assistance. He is responsible for using credit wisely and constructively. His day-to-day contact with firms in the same or allied trades all over the country keeps him up to date on the credit performance of many small and large firms. In addition to financial and credit advice, he can also offer assistance in purchasing and inventory controls, and he may even be a source of general information on activities within the trade. He may make occasional visits to the firm; but more important is his immediate availability by phone or through correspondence. Credit counsel such as this is offered by many large firms *at no cost* to the firms they supply.

Credit and collection skills can be improved by attending financial workshops and by reading current literature on the subject. Workshops are given by local credit organizations, universities, trade associations, and other educational groups. Any number of publications are available through organizations or libraries, or from publishers.

Summary

The management of credit and collections is vital to the success or failure of a small firm. With growing use of credit in business, the owner-manager must know how best to manage credit and collections. And if he doesn't know, he must learn.

Ability to understand and use credit can reduce pressures on the firm's need for working capital. This is particularly important for rapidly expanding firms having a thin capital base. When the small firm must extend credit to meet or beat a competitor, demands for capital will increase, as will overhead and the risks involved in credit and collection management. Understanding how to get low-cost financing for such activities can mean the difference between profit and loss for a firm.

As a firm grows, and extends more credit, it must have records and systems and procedures for credit management. Manufacturing or wholesaling firms with 20 or 25 major customers face a different problem from the retail store that has 3,000 to 4,000 consumer accounts. But in any case, as each operation grows, more formal record keeping must be developed, installed, and maintained.

The owner-manager must determine *when* to set up the new records, systems, and procedures. He must also instruct and direct his staff in the elements of credit and collection management. Without the manager's interest and discipline, the firm runs the risk of very serious bad-debt losses and lost customers.

Knowhow and experience in credit and collection management can be bolstered by the intelligent use of outside financial and credit organizations—such as credit bureaus, credit executives of supplier firms, and other businessmen.

Chapter 6

PURCHASING AND INVENTORY MANAGEMENT

VOLUME and type of purchasing among businesses vary widely depending upon the type of business. In wholesale and retail firms, goods purchased for resale are a vital part of the operations. In a manufacturing company, the importance of purchasing may vary; but it is still one of the owner-manager's important considerations. In a service business (such as a coin-operated laundry), purchasing may be a negligible factor.

Using Materials Management to Increase Profits

Materials management—the purchase of materials used, and the control and maintenance of inventories—is one of the most important tasks in almost any small firm. A large percentage of the owner-manager's sales dollar and his capital is invested in the purchase of raw materials, goods to be resold, parts, shop and office supplies, machinery and equipment, and the service of electricians, carpenters, plumbers, painters, and others. The efficiency with which the owner-manager does his buying may well determine his margin of profit.

Evaluating Purchasing and Inventory Management

The owner-manager should evaluate his purchasing procedures to learn: (1) how his material and service costs compare with those of his competitors; (2) whether his investment in inventory is too great; and (3) the true rate of his firm's inventory obsolescence. In addition, he must also objectively assess company losses from spoilage and pilferage. Management of inventories, whether large or small, requires some thought and control by the owner-manager or his keymen. Good inventory control can reduce loss resulting from spoilage, shrinkage, errors, and pilferage. In many firms, it can mean the difference between profit and loss.

Raw materials and work-in-process inventories enable people and machines to keep working. Parts inventories feed production and assembly lines. Finished goods inventories satisfy customers needs in manufacturing, distribution, and retailing.

The object of purchasing and inventory control is to have the proper goods in the right quantities at the right time and place and at the right cost. Having the goal of increasing his sales and profits, the owner-manager will want to give a great deal of study and thought to his purchasing and inventory program. The rate of turnover is a factor in determining the amount of management time that should be spent on purchasing and inventory control. For example, consider the situation of Melvin Stein, a wholesale produce distributor.

Stein Bros. Co., an Eastern firm, buys most of its produce directly from farmers in various parts of the country. Buyers represent the firm in the scattered local communities. Some of these communities are on the West Coast, and delivery to the East takes about 8 days —a considerable time for perishable products. Because of this long lag between purchase and delivery, the company is forced to speculate a great deal on prices.

Practice varies with the season of the year and with the current buying habits of customers, but purchases must usually be made long in advance of sales. Stein Bros. sells to grocery supermarkets, institutions, and other wholesalers. Demand for any particular produce commodity varies continuously—depending on the quality of the product when it arrives in the East and the amount of the same commodity available from other suppliers.

Daily closing inventories must be taken because each salesman must know how much of specific lots and items is available for sale the next morning. The inventory is used to check out the sales for every case or bushel received in each railroad car or truck, Stein Bros. knows

exactly how much profit is made on any given purchase. With an inventory turnover every 2 to 3 days (about 2 turnovers per week or 100 per year), the Stein Bros. office staff must always be on its toes to keep pace with changing market conditions.

A wholesale produce firm has quite a different problem from that of a TV service store or a retail furniture business, which might have turnover only 4 to 5 times per year. Turnover in manufacturing firms can vary from rapid (food firms) to slow (steel fabricators).

Every owner-manager should recognize the importance of materials management. A look at the ratio of cost of materials to sales is illustrative: Many wholesalers would show a ratio of 80 to 85 percent; for a retail store, the figure might be 60 to 65 percent; and for a manufacturer, 25 to 50 percent.

Increasing Profits Through Better Materials Management

Knowing the relative importance of purchasing and inventories to the firm, the owner-manager should then determine how he can improve profits through better materials management. A fresh look may point the way to opportunities for increased sales, better cash flow, and increased profitability. Reviewing previous requirements and current needs should be the basis for developing a program for the future.

If a manufacturer, the owner-manager can consider the advantages of "making" rather than "buying" items that are increasingly used. He might consider the values of working with other firms in a voluntary or cooperative buying group. He might change the policy of buying in large volume, or he might switch from many sources of supply to a single source. These or other changes could help him achieve lower costs, better inventory backup, exclusive representation of certain product lines, more technical management assistance, or possible longer terms of payment. In any event, planning and carrying out a program of materials management usually offer a host of practical values.

In examining his past management of purchasing and inventory, the owner manager must study the turnover of his various kinds of inventory. Such a review can be by type, by product line, or by supplier.

The owner-manager must pay particular attention to the continuing addition of new items and to the failure to chop off obsolete ones. Fear of showing a loss because of inventory write offs is short sighted. The day of reckoning always arrives. Delays in shaping a realistic inventory policy can seriously impair the firm's actual profit picture.

The problem of overstatement of inventory values may be just as bad for the firm as understatement of inventory values. Jack Troup's retail business paint is a case in point.

For many years, Troup's Paint provided a substantial living for Jack and his family. In the last two years, the price of paints became more competitive in his trading area. In addition, a number of new types of paints were introduced by each of his two major suppliers.

Suddenly, Jack found himself unable to meet and discount his trade debt. Sales increased over the prior year, but at a lower price level with resulting lower gross profits. Troup's inventory of paint had expanded to the point where it was difficult to move around in the warehouse. In the face of a tight cash situation, Jack called in his firm's long-time accountant to see if he could help determine what was happening. (As a rule, the accountant appeared only on an annual basis to prepare the tax returns).

The accountant called for an inventory count. In prior years he had little to do with the taking of the inventory. However, he did spot-check the pricing of the inventory. On this inventory-taking, the accountant worked through the week-end with Jack and three helpers. To Jack's dismay, he found a great deal of very old inventory in addition to an excess inventory of paint which had been basic until the new types were recently introduced. The new lines of paint were also heavily stocked because of the introductory deals that were offered.

The accountant realized that the level of inventory shown on the books was very conservative. The current inventory, having been carefully audited, reflected the most accurate value of the value of the firm's stock. The profit and loss statement showed that the firm appeared to be operating at break-even or a slight loss. The accountant noted that he would not be able to give Jack an accurate picture until another audited inventory was taken which would be consistent with the one just taken. He did say that the inventory must be greatly reduced so that the company's cash position would be improved. He suggested the possibility of making deals with certain suppliers for taking old goods for credit. He thought some suppliers might accept a deal whereby for each new order placed they might take back an equal amount of older stock until a more balanced inventory position was attained.

Jack Troup was also faced with some major changes in merchandising. His competition was very aggressive and sold at lower prices. As a result, Jack spoke with

each of his two major suppliers. One resource was extremely helpful in showing Jack how to meet the competitive situation. Jack was able to get a lower price from this supplier in addition to many merchandising aids by giving this resource the largest part of his business. The inventory of the second, and by then minor resource, was reduced to a very low point. Troup's Paint Store had gone through a difficult period and was able to survive. Troup's was changed from a conservative retail paint store to an aggressive merchandiser. The firm continued to improve its market position and Jack's concepts on buying and merchandising were sharpened as a result of this experience. He worked closely with his resources and kept in touch with new product developments in the field so that his firm would not be caught off guard again.

A Planned Purchasing Program

Estimates of a firm's materials requirements should not be based on outright guesses, but on adequate information. They should be specific, naming type, quality, brand, size or other characteristics necessary to identify a part, raw material, factory or office supply item, or finished product. The current inventory of each item being used should be precisely known.

In most instances it is important to control closely only those items having large dollar value. For example, a tire distributor must keep accurate records of his stock of tires because the average value at cost is very high. At the same time, he may not find it worthwhile to keep records on his stock of hubcaps because they have such low dollar value. A purchase history record may be enough. (The owner-manager must make a common-sense decision about the items on which he will keep close watch.)

Purchasing Requirements and Records

Regardless of dollar value, materials purchased for production or resale must be controlled. If the owner-manager is interested in maintaining low costs, purchasing cannot be left to chance. A purchasing system must be developed as the firm grows, particularly when the owner-manager begins to delegate authority and responsibility for procurement. Even if the boss establishes a price level with his suppliers, day-to-day handling of requisitions, buying, followup, receiving, checking, and paying for materials calls for sound procedures.

A purchasing system in a fast-moving small firm should have the following characteristics:

1. It should fill material needs quickly, easily, and accurately.
2. It should be simple and basic.
3. It should have definite, clear, and understandable procedures that would enable the owner-manager to avoid costly duplication and error.
4. It should fix responsibility for each step in purchasing; tasks would be divided among the receiver, the bookkeeper, and the person doing the buying and followup.
5. It should be able to handle either increasing or decreasing needs for materials. (This would affect the design of forms as well as the delegation of responsibilities.)

To keep from losing receiving records and to avoid pilferage in the receiving department, a serialized prenumbered receiving record system can be used. The forms may be issued from a register or from prenumbered notebooks. Generally, one copy is kept in the receiving department, and the second copy travels with the materials or is sent to the office. Keeping the records in numerical order automatically files them by date. When the receiving office informs the buyer that the goods have been received, its copy can be given to the bookkeeper to prepare for payment when the invoice is received. The bookkeeper can then file the office copy of the receiving report numerically, thus making certain that every receiving department report gets to the office. This avoids confusion in the office and keeps everyone in the receiving department on their toes because they have to verify goods received by signing the report.

Knowing his firm's purchasing requirements and the kind of systems and procedures required, the owner-manager can prevent many profit leaks and much confusion. The possibilities for losses through error, pilferage, and shrinkage are many. Following established systems and procedures can be an effective control.

A Purchasing Program Can Lower Costs of Goods Sold

In a great number of small firms, profits are restricted by the pricing policies of competitors. Frequently, the owner-manager will either cut his selling prices or offer additional services at the same selling price; both have the effect of lowering his gross profits. Then he may resort to a successive reduction in expenses—concentrating on cutting overhead in order to survive the pressure of lowered gross profits.

While this approach is usually realistic and practical, it may not be the proper strategy for all situations. If materials consumed are a high percentage of the firm's selling dollar, then a good alternative would be to develop a program to lower the cost of goods sold. In retail and wholesale firms, the cost of goods sold is high; in manufacturing firms, it will vary depending upon the trade, and in service firms, it will depend upon the type of firm—from high in filling stations to low in laundromats.

If the owner-manager can meet his competition through a hard-hitting attack on the cost of goods sold, he may be able not only to lower costs, but also to develop new approaches to his marketing.

A well-thought-out purchasing program would include:

1. Determining past, present, and expected rates of usage of materials.
2. Keeping abreast of changes by suppliers in quality, price, delivery, and technology.
3. Determining suppliers' ability to maintain backup inventories.
4. Considering new products or materials that new suppliers, domestic or foreign, may be offering.
5. Learning of possible special deals for merchandise that the firm's major suppliers might be offering in other parts of the country or to competitors; also checking for special dating terms.
6. Determining the availability of factory specials, closeouts, or end-of-season runs.
7. Assessing the value of exclusive buying arrangements (for retailers and wholesalers) which could be an important marketing advantage.
8. Considering group buying arrangements with other small firms.
9. Using the services of buying offices where available.

It takes time to investigate the many possible ways to improve purchasing. With a plan, the owner-manager can go about it effectively. A plan is essential when the owner-manager's under pressure. It will help him to concentrate on the elements that present the greatest opportunity.

Inventory Management

A large part of most firms' capital frequently is tied up in inventory. Using this inventory to make profits depends on the owner-manager's attitude toward good inventory management. One measure of effective inventory management is the inventory ratio: the cost of goods sold for a year divided by the average value of the inventory. The higher the turnover, the more untied is the inventory. Sometimes, however, inventories are kept too low, and too many sales are lost as a result. The owner-manager must strive for the proper balance. Each turnover gives him gross profit on the goods sold; and the more frequent the turnover, the more gross profits. This is analogous to taking the cream off the top of a bottle of milk: The more bottles of milk that are sold, the more fat there is to take off.

Systems and Records

The owner-manager who seeks better inventory management should:

1. Develop a system with procedures appropriate to the importance and size of inventories.
2. Maintain appropriate records on the firm's basic inventory transactions.
3. Establish and maintain effective receiving, inspection, stocking, picking or issuing, and shipping operations.
4. Locate inventories so that inventory-taking can be accomplished conveniently.

The basic information required from inventory control systems and records is of the following kinds:

1. *Demand:* A record of orders or sales.
2. *Purchases:* a history of resources, prices, order cycles, and quantities.
3. *Receipts:* Quantities, delivery cycle, and returned goods.
4. *Issuance:* rate of internal use or specific delivery data.

All four kinds of information may not be required in every situation. For example, a manufacturing firm that operates from an instock position of finished goods would not require demand figures because the issuance record would be satisfactory. However, all four pieces of information would be required if the specific part is used in manufacturing one or more of the company's products.

In a small wholesale firm, it may be necessary to maintain only a purchase and receipts record. Amounts used of specific items can be determined by adding receipts to the beginning inventory and subtracting the ending inventory figure. The figures derived in this approach merely indicate the quantity of an item that has been used. It doesn't offer much protection against pilferage and waste. Whatever system is used requires a periodic review.

Control Procedures. Inventory control is usually handled through observation, physical checks, and perpetual inventory records, or a combination of these. (In merchandising, both dollar control and unit control systems will be needed.)

Most small firms initiate inventory control through "observation" and "memory." The careful opening and closing of the firm's doors is either handled by the owner-manager or is delegated to a trusted employee.

A physical inventory check of the entire stock requires a great deal of time for an accurate count and must be done during nonworking periods. Its value in controlling items or product lines will vary according to the size and type of inventory. A system of inventory credits is a useful alternative. In this setup, a "bonding," or inventory record, card is placed in the bin holding a particular item. The stockman, noting that he has reached a minimum level for some item, sends its bonding card to the office to request reorder. The inventory bonding card has all the necessary data for reordering the item.

Many firms check their stock by product lines or by sources. Sometimes, supplier salesmen take periodic or annual inventories of their own lines. This saves time for the owner-manager and reviews the stock for proper balance.

Perpetual inventories, which seek to keep a running tally on the current stock of an item, are attempted by many small firms; but they are rarely accurate and really up to date. They are most successful in the control of high-dollar-value items. Such items receive a great deal of management attention; hence, the organization is disciplined to keep close watch on them and the control is more apt to be accurate. Even here, goods allocated or sold and still in stock can be a problem if not properly marked. The true test of the value of a perpetual, inventory system is the willingness of a member of the firm to promise delivery on the strength of the inventory record. Very often, a call or a trip to the stockroom is necessary before any such promise can be given. (Perpetual records of purchases and receipts are also often used; they do not have to be posted on every demand or issue of the item, and thus tend to be more accurate and of real value.)

Once a system is established, its true operating value to the owner-manager will vary according to the amount of interest, attention, and discipline that he applies to it. As the firm grows, the systems will naturally become more detailed because more people will be involved. However, even then, the owner-manager's continuing interest is the chief guarantee that the systems will serve the intended purposes.

Effective Inventory Management

Establishing a good system and set of inventory records is important, but policies on all phases of purchasing and inventory must be regularly reviewed. For example, a retailer's reliance on a long-time relationship with a specific supplier for a given product line can lead to trouble. The supplier's real value to the firm may have dropped if new products or fresh merchandising ideas have been developed by other sources. Relationships with reliable suppliers are important, but market conditions must not be ignored.

The owner manager must pay particular attention to the items he adds to and drops from his inventory. Change is continuous, and the owner-manager must try to eliminate older stocks of a given item before replacements are offered for sale. Failure to do so will make the left-over inventory worthless.

The opportunity to "make" instead of "buy" is important to manufacturers when the volume requirements of a certain commodity reach the proper economic levels. (It can affect the wholesaler and retailer too. They may be able to use private-label merchandise rather than branded merchandise when their volume is sufficiently high.) The small manufacturer must realize that, in many cases, he represents the "buy" side of his larger customer's procurement policy. And in many cases his own firm may be better off buying certain components or items from firms specially equipped to produce them than it would be in trying to manufacture them. Screws and nuts are a good example. Specialized equipment and know-how enable screw and nut manufacturers to turn out standard items at a unit cost vastly lower than could those who buy from them.

Many small firms enter new fields by buying a product and perhaps relabeling it or making the final assembly. Actual production is deferred until sales reach a profitable volume.

These are but a few of the situations the owner-manager may encounter. In each of them, it is important that he recognize the values of establishing *balanced* policies for inventory management. Operating hit or miss leads to a tremendous duplication of effort, and the building of large, uncontrolled inventories. Yet, the owner-manager who buys his annual requirements at one time (without perhaps quite knowing what they are) because of a special offer of a low price is also indulging in an approach that is very lax, dangerous, and potentially costly.

Controlling Materials

Materials can be lost through pilferage, shrinkage, errors, or waste. Because management is so close to operations in the small firm, unnecessary waste of materials can usually be avoided. But as a firm grows, and authority and responsibility are delegated to employees, interest in reducing material losses may decrease. At this point, the owner-manager must decide on the best way to organize the use and handling of materials.

The owner-manager should hold on to responsibility for purchasing high-dollar-value items until the firm is large enough to support the services of a purchasing agent. Responsibility for buying less expensive items can be delegated. An occasional audit will indicate if directions are being carried out.

Continuous Audit. The control of goods received from suppliers requires a continuous audit. Many forms of pilferage can occur in the receiving department. The quantity and kind of commodity are identified there before being sent to stock or shipped to a customer. And payment of the vendor's invoice is based upon the receiving report.

Operating a stockroom or warehouse involves a great deal of control. Goods must be stored where they are supposed to be; they must be easily found when required; and any goods issued must have bonafide authorization. Particularly to be avoided are: lost goods, which necessitates duplication of inventory; and poor handling, which causes damage and breakage.

The day-to-day security of the warehouse—especially during coffee breaks, lunchtimes, and off hours—requires attention as does the screening of employees coming and going.

Checking Daily Shipments. Checking daily shipments—by company trucks, common carrier, or customer's vehicle—for proper documentation is a vital part of material control. Using serialized prenumbered forms for shipping memorandums and bills of lading will help reduce losses in the shipping room.

Every step from purchasing to shipping requires the services of trained and trusted employees. Specific people must be given responsibilities in every phase. They must be responsible for the material they are using and handling. The manager must establish the necessary systems, procedures, records, and forms so that everyone involved with materials will know what is going on at all times. The case of Wyman Paper Distributors, Inc., shows what can happen.

Mike Wyman, with the help of a reliable group of key subordinates in the warehouse and office, had managed his firm profitably for more than 15 years. During the last 2 years, however, profits had not been as high as expected.

The firm purchased large rolls of paper from many mills in carload quantities, and then processed them into many products. Routinely checking yields on bulk paper purchases, the firm's auditors found that processing shrinkage had increased about 50 percent since the previous audit, 5 years earlier.

Because new equipment designed to reduce processing losses had been added after the last audit, the firm's records for the preceding 3 years were checked, and it was discovered that losses had begun to increase about 2 years ago. Shop operations were reviewed and everything appeared in order; losses measured daily and weekly were as calculated.

By accident, a clerk, while checking a production lot in the shop in the absence of the bookkeeper, discovered that some rolls were missing from a given mill lot. Further investigation revealed that rolls of paper were being stolen systematically. The firm's receiver, its bookkeeper, and one of its truckers (who carried the rolls from a distant railroad siding to the warehouse) were operating as a team. The trucker would sell a given number of rolls from each shipment; the receiver would report all rolls as being received, and because he also issued rolls to production, he would account for the missing rolls. The bookkeeper had discovered what was going on shortly after the ring began operating and had been persuaded to join the other two.

Had the owner-manager kept a closer watch on operations and had the firm's auditors been asked earlier to check this important part of material consumption, the losses might possibly have been discovered sooner. Had the bookkeeper known that, as a matter of policy, his work would be regularly checked by the owner-manager and the auditors, he would probably have reported the problem at the outset instead of getting involved.

Stealing is apt to go on in any business. The only question is "How much?" It is up to the owner-manager to keep theft —as well as waste and shrinkage of materials—under control Most owner-managers recognize the dangers of stock shortages and their effect on invested capital; but often they must discipline themselves and others to reduce material losses. General steps that most owner-managers can take to hold down such losses are the following:

1. Encourage close employer-employee relationships.
2. Set a good example by not taking materials from firm.
3. Investigate new employees carefully.
4. Check on suspicious activities of older employees.
5. Tighten up systems and records dealing with receiving, issuance, and shipping of goods.
6. Keep warehouse orderly and clean.
7. Instruct auditor to make unannounced material checks.
8. Provide reasonable security against customer and employee pilferage.
9. Keep tight control over keys and over the opening and closing of shop and office.

The Well-Disciplined Organization

Many an owner-manager feels that by making a good purchase he has already made his profits. In most instances, he couldn't be more wrong. Products must be shipped, received, processed or put into stock, rehandled, packed for shipment, and delivered to the customer in the proper quantity and condition before any profits result. And many of these steps between purchase and delivery provide opportunities for errors in description, handling, marking and physical damage. Only a trained, well-disciplined organization—perhaps just one or two people in a small firm—can handle the many steps in an orderly fashion. Without such an organization, no owner-manager can be sure of making the expected profits on his purchases.

The steps in materials management—

Buying
Expediting
Receiving
Inspecting
Dispatching
Shipping
Trucking—can be handled in a very small firm by the warehouse boss, the shipper, or the production foreman. As the firm grows, each step will require supervision by one or more persons.

With greater workload and the addition of personnel, the owner-manager will need to change systems and procedures used. He must also be prepared to train new people to perform the specific functions. A newly hired "shipper" who had the same title in another firm could have been doing an entirely different job there.

Good organization and systems are merely the foundation upon which to build a successful materials management program. Continued supervision is needed. With proper discipline the small firm can avoid many losses common to large firms and can compete successfully. The owner-manager's dedication to controlling purchasing and inventories can bring handsome rewards in increased profits.

Summary

Purchasing and inventory management are very important to owner-managers of most small firms. Relating the cost of materials consumed to the data on the firm's profit-and-loss statement readily shows its importance. As a result, the owner-manager will probably want to develop a materials purchasing and inventory program. He can either spend more of his own time handling it or can delegate it to a key subordinate.

The purchasing responsibility should include locating resources, negotiating terms, following up on deliveries, and making certain of the quality of goods received. Large suppliers may be induced to extend special terms and services beneficial to the small firm. These terms and services may include lower prices for concentration of purchases, extended credit, warehousing back-up, technical product assistance and training, and general management and merchandising aids.

A systematic purchasing program requires systems and procedures in addition to the necessary records and files. Since everything purchased must be received, used or resold, and paid for, more than one person is invariably involved. To avoid wasted time, confusion, and errors, the owner-manager must decide which are the best ways of setting up the necessary systems. When major changes occur, these systems and records must be reviewed.

Each step in the control of materials—receiving goods, placing them into stock, processing materials, storing goods, picking, packing, shipping, and trucking finished goods to ultimate customers—represents a source of potential damage or loss. Therefore, the owner-manager must establish specific responsibilities among his employees for such functions as receiving, warehousing, and shipping. As these persons handle the goods, each should keep his part of a record that can be used to trace problem situations.

Actual inventory control is exercised by observation, physical checks, or by perpetual inventory records. In small firms, observation and physical checks through such systems as max-min bin control are commonly used. For high-dollar items such as tires or appliances, perpetual inventory records are necessary. Perpetual inventory record cards which show "on hand" balances are seldom accurate enough. When used, these cards generally show demand or sales, purchase history, record of parts or goods receipts and issuances or shipments. The owner-manager must decide which particular type of inventory control system is best for his firm.

The owner-manager should aim at having sufficient inventory of goods and supplies to satisfy his firm's needs for effective low-cost production or "in-stock" needs of finished goods of his customers. Balancing the inventory among product lines, types of materials, and resources so as to attain effective use of the firm's capital requires a great deal of information-seeking and forethought. Success is measured by the inventory turnover of a firm compared with that of similar firms. The owner-manager of a small firm can often exert more effective inventory control than can his larger competitors. His closeness to purchasing, to his customers, and to his warehouse and shop helps him to maintain a close grasp of the entire situation. But he can do this only if he recognizes its importance and is willing to do the job.

Chapter 7

ACCOUNTING AND STATISTICS–BUDGETING AND EXPENSE CONTROL

WITHOUT accurate, current information, well-reasoned business decisions simply cannot be made. The owner-manager must be aware of this. He must also recognize that, as his firm grows, he will have to stop depending only on his memory. He must set up a system for compiling, recording, and analyzing the business data he needs.

Importance of Accounting and Statistical Information

The accounting and statistical information needed by a firm will vary with the size of the firm, amount of trade it has, and the ability of the owner-manager to use such information. An accounting system can:

1. Report information on the firm's operating results.
2. Provide a basis for comparing current performance with the previous year's operating results and with forecasted targets.

3. Provide the figures for the firm's operating statement and balance sheet.
4. Aid the preparation of reports and tax returns for government regulatory and tax-collecting agencies.

The Management Information System

The development and the use of good records are essential. Time after time, reviews of bankrupt small firms show that they failed to maintain adequate records. Up-to-date, accurate, and proper records act as *sensing* devices for the owner-manager, helping him to carry out more effective planning and control. Good records can highlight sales by area, man, and product; they can reveal material waste, employee frauds, spoilage, and errors; and they can pinpoint cash position and numerous other vital business facts.

Accounting System Procedures. Every firm needs an accounting system to safeguard business assets and prevent errors. It should be accurately and honestly maintained, *transaction by transaction,* by those keeping the books. A system of checks and balances should be installed so that no employee will have complete control of any given business transaction. Employees handling cash should not be allowed to keep the books of account. Those working as cashiers or collecting accounts should not also be doing bookkeeping. The employee authorizing purchases should be someone other than the bookkeeper.

Where possible, records analyses and reports should be the responsibility of at least two people. For example, employee earnings under piece rates should be computed by one clerk and checked for accuracy by another. Cash register tapes should be used to double check the cash received by the cashier.

The Bookkeeping Process. The bookkeeping process (as shown in figure 10) is based on:

Original documents that record transactions when they are made. Examples of such documents would include sales slips, receiving records, invoices, checks, employee time cards, and the like.

Journals that are formal "books of original entry." These would record transactions in chronological order and the debits and credits involved. In addition to a general journal, there may be one or more special journals for particular kinds of transactions. Common kinds of journals include those for sales, purchasing, and cash.

Figure 10—The Bookkeeping Process

ORIGINAL RECORDS (BUSINESS PAPERS)
(Sales slips, receiving records, invoices, checks, etc.)
JOURNALS
(General journals, sales journal, purchase journal, cash book, etc.)
LEDGER
(Accounts for each asset, liability and capital items, expenses and revenues)
TRIAL BALANCE
(List of net amount or **balance** in each account)
FINANCIAL STATEMENTS
(Balance sheet, profit-and-loss statement, others)

The *ledger*. To make the information recorded in the journal more useable, each item is later transferred, or posted, to a ledger account. An account is a record of the increases and decreases in one type of asset, liability, capital, income, or expense. A book or file in which a number of accounts are kept together is called a ledger.

Trial balances that make certain all the entries in the ledger are in balance and in good order. The trial balance should be taken as close to the end of a period as possible.

Financial statements that are prepared once the trial balance is taken. For most small firms, it is important to have statement information within the first 10 days of the following month.

Information Needed. Typical kinds of information that the owner-manager must have to manage effectively include facts and figures on marketing, operations, and finances. Information on *marketing* (*or sales*) should include: activities of outside and inside salesmen, shipment information, selling expenses, gross profit and pricing figures, and advertising and sales promotion data. Information on *operations,* should include: purchasing (buying), inventory, packing and shipping, order processing and production scheduling, industrial engineering and tooling, employee relations, and cost analysis. Information on *financial and accounting* can be obtained through balance sheets, profit-and-loss statements, ratios of P & L statement items to balance sheet items, and statements of working capital finds.

To manage a firm effectively, the owner-manager must have certain data hourly, daily, or weekly. Some of this information, such as analysis of sales slips or invoices, may later be fed into the regular accounting process. But the owner-manager will not be fully in control if he waits for monthly, quarterly, or annual accounting reports and meanwhile operates "by the seat of his pants." Most managers of small firms have a "feel" for what is going on in all aspects of their operations; and when this feel is supported by simple, accurate, up-to-date facts, their decision-making fares even better.

Organizing Accounting Information

The hard-working owner-manager is deeply involved in the operations of his business. Why should he need to organize the information he already knows? Wouldn't he be better off spending his time "doing" rather than sitting at a desk adding up figures? If this is his attitude, the owner-manager must try to understand: 1) what is meant by information; 2) where it is developed; 3) how he can use it; and 4) what is required to put it into organized written form. He must try to overcome his personal lack of interest or knowhow. And he should consider using the part-time services of outside bookkeepers, accountants, or consultants to help develop and operate an effective program. If he depends solely upon himself, he will tend to avoid the manual tasks involved with recordkeeping; and, as a result, he will make little or no progress.

Budgeting and Expense Controls

Too frequently an owner-manager will fail to work with budgeting and expense controls. Unfortunately, it takes more than a busy store and a successful sales force to make a profit; it also takes administrative control of sales revenue and business expenses.

With an understanding of budgeting and forecasting, the owner-manager can compare his current operations to his forecast or budget; and he can then set up a continuing plan of action that will help him meet or improve his forecast.

Daily pressures on the owner-manager come from many sources. He faces major and minor decisions at the same time. Unfortunately, too many owner-managers give the same amount of thought and study to both. When the owner-manager recognizes this imbalance, he may consider changing the way he manages his time and the way he manages his business.

The "seat of the pants" approach to decision-making brings on a host of problems. It results in frustration for the owner-manager and his employees. And this, in turn, can lead to a high turnover of employees and a retarded growth rate for the firm.

The mere fact that an owner-manager spends a lot of his personal time in trying to make his business a success is no guarantee that he is going to succeed. How can he run his business effectively? At the same time, how can he develop an information system that will highlight weaknesses in the firm? How can he direct his skills and those of his employees into the proper channels? The answer to these questions is the installation and understanding of budgeting, expense control, and forecasting—of the types that are most applicable to his firm. Being able to distinguish his major problems will give the owner time to concentrate his energies on them and deal with them effectively.

Preparing a Budget

The ultimate target being a higher net profit, not just increased sales, the owner-manager must first determine what gross profit and expenses will be.

Preparing a budget even for a very small firm, is not a one-man job. Key subordinates, bookkeeper, accountant—all have their part to contribute.

The First Planning Meeting. A planning meeting with all present, should be held to discuss the previous year's actual sales and operating expenses; and new projects or additional expenses for the coming year should be brought up for consideration. Each area of sales and expense should be assigned to the appropriate person. For example, maintenance and repairs would be the responsibility of the shop foreman; expenses for office supplies would be the responsibility of the bookkeeper. A number of the expense items would be the direct responsibility of the owner himself. Each person would study the previous year's figures and develop, in time for the next meeting, a breakdown (by months or by quarters) of the coming year's expected spending (using a form such as shown in figure 11) after a sales budget has been determined.

At this point, the owner-manager *must* disclose certain operating figures to his keymen. There is some risk that this information will become general knowledge. However, it is

Figure 11—Expenses Forecast

Estimated Expenses for Coming Year (Use nearest dollar figures)

Expense Item	Actual This Year	Estimate Coming Year
PERSONNEL EXPENSES		
(Salaries, wages, bonuses)		
Executives	______	______
Office	______	______
Store	______	______
Salesmen	______	______
All other	______	______
OPERATING EXPENSES		
Advertising and catalogs		
Bad debts	______	______
Cash discounts allowed	______	______
Delivery (Oil, gas, repairs)	______	______
Depreciation	______	______
Donations	______	______
Dues and subscriptions	______	______
Employee benefits	______	______
Heat, light, power, and water	______	______
Insurance	______	______
Interest	______	______
Legal and auditing	______	______
Maintenance and repairs		
Office supplies	______	______
Outboard freight	______	______
Postage (except parcel post)	______	______
Rent (or equivalent)	______	______
Sales expense (entertainment and travel)	______	______
Shipping and store room supplies	______	______
Taxes	______	______
Telephone and telegraph	______	______
All other	______	______
TOTAL ESTIMATED EXPENSES		$______
TOTAL ACTUAL EXPENSES	$______	

very important to get the cooperation of the firm's keymen. With "the facts," not only will they develop a feeling of "belonging," but they may also make some practical and expense-saving contributions. They should be dealt with individually or in small groups. As the keymen learn how to handle confidential company information, the owner-manager can disclose more to them. In most very small firms, the keymen will be "working" bosses. Chances are their participation in the internal workings of the firm will strengthen both their attitude and their performance.

The Second Planning Meeting. At a second planning meeting, the owner-manager, the bookkeeper, and the accountant, consulting with the foreman or the department heads, should work out a forecast of expenses in each department for every month of the year, based upon the forecasted sales program. Any special projects that are planned can be noted on the budget for the month in which the expense is to be incurred. In this way, an accumulation of costs related to the special project can be controlled. In some cases, special project expenses will be listed on a separate sheet and only the final total will be noted on the master budget.

Once the proper expense classifications are established, the bookkeeper can routinely post the "actual" monthly expenses on the expense control (figure 12). To be of real value, the report should be ready immediately at the end of the month. If the bookkeeper faces special problems and gets behind, the owner-manager will have to get additional help.

Forecast and Budget. Business forecasting, based on past and current experience, helps the owner-manager to develop a strategy based upon the various opportunities available to the firm at a given time. This may be done by consulting industry trends or past records. Forecasting is more effective when figures are as specific as possible. For example, a forecast of a 10-percent increase in sales for the year has some value; but it would be more helpful if the expected increase were shown for each month.

A forecast of sales and costs is the foundation upon which to build an effective budgeting program. With it, the owner-manager and his keymen can prepare the expense budget needed to accomplish the goals set forth. Then actual expenses can be compared with estimated expenses for each account classification.

Unexpected events are always occurring in a dynamic small business. Of what value, then, is a written forecast of sales and expenses that will be constantly changing? The value is this: a forecast of sales and expenses is developed, then deviations can be quickly spotted, and their positive or negative effects on the business can be evaluated.

Figure 12—Monthly Expense Budget (Estimated and Actual)

	January			February			March		
	Est.	Actual	Over/ under	Est.	Actual	Over/ under	Est.	Actual	Over/ under
PERSONNEL									
Executives									
Office									
Store									
Salesman									
All others									
OPERATING									
Advertising and catalogs									
Bad debts									
Cash discount allowed									
Delivery (oil, gas, repair)									
Depreciation									

Donations									
Dues and subscriptions									
Employee benefits									
Heat, light, power, and water									
Insurance									
Interest									
Legal and auditing									
Maintenance and repairs									
Office supplies									
Outboard freight									
Postage (except parcel post)									
Rent or equivalent									
Sales expense (entertainment and travel)									
Shipping and store room									
Supplies									
Taxes									
Telephone and telegraph									
All others									

If the firm has a 2-year budget in which next year's estimates are broken down by months and in which the second year's estimates are broken down by quarters, then the owner-manager and his keymen will be inclined to look ahead and plan accordingly.

Some time ago, at the urging of his accountant and a business consultant, Gordon Shalek, owner-manager of Shalek Jewelry Manufacturing Co., decided to make his firm's first 12-month budget. At the outset, Gordon thought it would be a waste of time because he had been running his business for 30 years; he thought he had all the information he needed; and sales had been growing about 25 percent annually during the past 3 years.

Working with his accountant and the consultant, Gordon reviewed sales and expenses, by account classifications, for the previous 3 years. The three then developed ratios of the expenses to sales for each category, discovering that some expense items were relatively fixed. After they reviewed annual figures, they made a month-to-month review because the firm's high selling period in July and August was matched by a high shipping period in November and December. Lowest sales occurred in December and January, and lowest shipping loads were in January, February, and March.

As a result of the analysis, several interesting conclusions became apparent. For example, some of the firm's production and shipping should be done in September and October, before the Christmas rush; to do this would reduce pressure on the shipping department and reduce the normally heavy volume of overtime in the shop. It would also allow the firm to take on some late reorder business in November and December.

Mr. Shalek also saw the need to create new incentives for his salesmen; he decided to add a special winter promotion to stimulate business during the January-March period. And he decided that certain employees should, if possible, take their vacations during this slow winter season.

After analyzing past experience, Gordon and the others forecast sales and expenses, by months, for the coming year—incorporating many of the ideas found in the earlier analysis. A new plan of operations was put into effect, and Gordon and his keymen set out to "beat the budget." They did, substantially increasing sales and reducing expenses, particularly during the slower periods.

The firm made a profit every month during the first year the budget was used. Special bonuses raised employee interest even higher; new policies were introduced with little resistance; and plans had to be made in January and February to expand the plant or lease additional space. Even with two shifts and a partial third shift, the plant could not produce the business expected in October, November, and December.

Using An Accounting Firm

The accountant has a vital role in the health of a business. Retaining one only to prepare an annual tax return fails to take advantage of his extensive business talents.

Some of the reasons commonly given for not using an accountant's services more effectively are the following:

1. Fee is too high.

2. Owner-manager is unwilling to disclose confidential transactions.

3. An independent examination of the firm's performance is not important because the manager is also the owner.

4. A trusted employee has always handled the firm's records.

5. The business is only a small one; and the owner-manager can use his own judgment as to how properly to value inventories, accounts receivable, plant and equipment, accounts payable and the net worth of the firm.

6. The firm's bank knows the business and will provide all the financing required without an audited financial statement.

7. The firm had an accountant for a number of years, and he didn't do anything that couldn't be done by someone else.

8. The firm's profitability is measured daily by the amount of "cash" available, so additional figures aren't considered necessary.

It is important that the owner-manager develop some sort of a standard against which he can compare his past experience with individual accounting firms.

What an Accountant Does

Services offered by public accountants generally include:

1. Preparing tax returns and planning tax programs.
2. Reviewing and developing a firm's accounting needs.
3. Assisting in the selection and training of a bookkeeping staff.
4. Advising on records and systems management.
5. Preparing financial statements (including the trial balance); also auditing records to safeguard a firm's assets.
6. Assisting in review and study of financial statements.
7. Helping determine a firm's cash flow and capital requirements.
8. Assisting in establishing budgets and expense controls.
9. Helping set up sound credit policies.
10. Providing purchasing and inventory controls.
11. Working with a firm's attorney and other professional consultants to provide sound financial management, draft of contracts and leases, and determine adequate insurance coverage.
12. Acting as a sounding board for the owner-manager.

The selection of a firm's accountant rests with the owner-manager. Once an accountant has been selected, his value usually increases as he becomes more familiar with the technical aspects of a business; from the start, however, he has a store of knowledge and experience in the administrative phases of business.

Many accounting firms get into a position with some of their clients where they merely perform routine accounting functions that represent a very small part of the services the owner-manager can actually use.

John Jaffe operates a wine distribution business which his father started many years ago. When his father died 4 years ago, John took over the management of the firm. It had been profitable over the years; but lately, profits had begun to decline because of increased expenses and greater competition.

Jaffe Wine Distributors used the services of an independent public accountant who prepared the firm's trial balance each month from the bookkeeper's postings. He had been the firm's accountant for 22 years and had gone through almost the same routine of coming in monthly and preparing the figures for John's father. The elder Jaffe had a good accounting background and could interpret the figures. He was also a very dynamic, and positive-acting manager. John, on the other hand, had little accounting experience, but he was a good salesman.

After receiving the accountant's figures for 6 months, and seeing the poor results they revealed, John hired an independent consulting firm to review his operations. The consultants found that expenses were getting out of line and that John was making too many sales at

reduced prices. The consultants recognized that John was weak in accounting and needed to improve in it. They also suggested that he consider making a different sort of arrangement with the firm's accountant. It was urged that the accountant, after he had prepared the monthly statements, sit down with John and point out the areas of strength and weakness.

As it turned out, John and the firm's accountant decided it would be best if Jaffe Wine Distributors were to hire another accounting firm that could offer the type of services that the accountant agreed the firm needed under John's management. John then called his banker and talked to some friends. He interviewed three accounting firms and eventually replaced the old accountant with one of these firms.

After working a year with the new accountant, John had reduced his firm's operating expenses and hired an additional salesman. The profit picture improved considerably and the accountant helped improve the firm's bank relationship. With a new and larger loan, Jaffe Distributors began discounting all its bills and developed some new credit policies unique for that trade—policies which allowed John to increase the firm's sales. During the first year, as a result of the efforts of the new accountant, John improved his own understanding of accounting and management controls. The progress made by the firm more than offset the slightly increased accounting fees.

Working with the Accountant

Many small firms are even more successful than they would otherwise be because their owner-managers have a long-time relationship with an outside independent accountant. Many owner-managers have a weak background in accounting, finance, and management controls; and the accountant, in addition to acting as an auditor and as a sounding board on major issues, is apt to ask pertinent questions that will keep the owner-manager alert and objective.

The owner-manager should try to meet at least once a month with his accountant after financial statements for the period have been prepared. Such meetings should be held where there will be no interruptions.

Performance in the previous month is compared with that of a year ago, then with the month preceding. Major deviations are discussed. Current month plans are discussed and then future plans and problems. Occasionally, the meeting includes some or all of the owner's keymen. The accountant's opinion and evaluation of the keymen's presentations will help the owner-manager make up his own mind.

Summary

The owner-manager must recognize the usefulness of information systems in his growing firm. An adequate current flow of internal and external information will aid him in making well-reasoned decisions. The owner-manager must learn to rely on factual data accumulated systematically. His reliance on rough facts taken from memory can be disastrous as he adds employees and assigns them responsibilities without the necessary backup information.

Good recordkeeping is a characteristic of successful business firms. The accounting system used should provide a clear picture of the firm's performance. The information generated should be reviewed monthly or quarterly. In addition to his own skills, the owner-manager can get assistance from his accountant, banker, lawyer, suppliers, and business friends.

The owner-manager should also develop budgeting and expense controls providing up-to-the-minute nonaccounting information to use in narrowing the time between a business action and his own reaction. Management control information is needed in areas such as sales, operations, and purchasing.

Because a good net profit is the target of any firm, close attention should be paid to expenses. Too frequently, owner-managers concentrate most of their efforts on sales alone. When he develops a forecast of sales, the owner-manager should also develop a budget of expenses for the same period. Then he will have a target to undershoot, if possible; and his monthly review of actual and estimated expenses will allow him to know exactly where his funds are being used.

Using public accountants will allow the owner-manager to take advantage of the many vital services they offer—particularly their assistance in administrative matters and in helping safeguard the firm's assets. By meeting with the accountant on a continuing basis and by having him available to discuss matters pertaining to current performance and future business strategies, many businessmen have avoided making serious business errors. Using the accountant as a sounding board will help the owner-manager to become a more effective manager.

Chapter 8

MANAGEMENT CONSIDERATIONS IN TAXATION

THE small businessman must be interested in taxation because it bears so directly on his success or failure. Tax laws are always changing, many times in ways which directly affect the owner-manager as he plans the future strategy of his business.

Understanding Tax Responsibilities

More and more management decisions require the owner-manager to have a broad knowledge of taxes. The continuing changes in taxes require the owner-manager to be alert to their effects. Because taxes affect almost every phase of business operations (see figure 13), the owner-manager must make decisions that avoid the pitfalls arising from poor knowledge of taxation.

When he faces tax questions, the owner-manager should remember the following:

First, taxes are only one of many factors that an owner-manager must consider in deciding on a certain course of action, and it may be that other factors are overriding.

Second, there is a vital difference between tax *evasion,* (the failure to pay taxes due) and tax *avoidance* (management of affairs in such a way as to lower tax liability). No taxpayer is required to organize his affairs in such a manner as to create maximum revenues for the Governmnt. It is quite legal to develop a business decision in such a form that the tax burden will be minimized.

Third, taxation is an extremely technical, complex, and changing subject—with frequent revision and a continual stream of Treasury decisions and litigated cases. When a tax problem appears to be developing, the owner-manager should seek guidance from a professional tax authority rather than attempt to solve the problem using hearsay and out-of-date opinions.

Tax Effects in Management Decisions

The owner-manager must recognize a tax problem and be able to make a judgment on it that will not hinder his firm's growth and progress. Business policies which are influenced by tax considerations would include:

Inventory—valuation, method, yearend purchasing and inventory reduction programs in relation to assessment dates.

Wages—tax effects, use of other employee incentives with different tax considerations, such as stock options, deferred payment, pension plans.

Sales—tax base, methods of payment.

Asset purchases—value of leasing program, rate of depreciation.

Financing—use of notes, tax-deductibility of expenses, investing equity capital.

Improper accumulation of earnings—corporation's dividend payments.

Capital gains and losses—timing of various capital transactions such as sale of assets, acquisition of firms, etc.

Accounts receivable—write-off experience, effect on credit policies.

Estate and gift—timing of disposition of business interests.

Tax Effects on Long-Range Plans

The long-range goals of the owner-manager of a small business are directly related to his tax planning. Does he plan to build the business and pass it along to his children? Does he plan to run it as successfully as he can and sell it when he

Figure 13—Kinds of Business Taxes

FEDERAL	Individual income taxes Corporate income taxes Excise taxes—manufacturers, retailers Employment taxes Social security taxes Death taxes Stamp taxes Occupational taxes Customs
STATE (SPECIFIC TAXES VARY IN EACH STATE)	Individual income taxes Corporate income taxes Gross receipts and sales taxes Business real and personal property taxes Capital stock taxes Business automobile and truck licenses, inspection fees Death taxes Foreign-state business taxes Workmen's compensation insurance premiums Incorporation fees Employment taxes
LOCAL	Individual income taxes Sales taxes City, school district, and county real and personal property taxes Business licenses Business real and personal property taxes

gets the best offer or when he plans to retire? Does he plan to hire others to run daily operations so that he can oversee more than one firm? These and similar questions should be answered or brought into clearer focus, for they are an important factor in any decision concerning the proper legal form for a business.

Legal Form of a Business. The owner-manager must choose between a sole proprietorship, partnership, or corporation. A sole proprietorship represents an individual for tax purposes; all business income is treated as income of the owner. Net business income is subject to taxation at individual tax rates.

A partnership, which is a legal entity for many purposes, is not so recognized for income taxation. Income from a partnership is declared on the partners' individual returns, where it is taxed at individual tax rates.

A corporation is recognized as a legal entity for tax purposes. After corporate earnings are taxed, the remaining profits (if not retained in the business) are passed on to stockholders, where they may be taxed once again as dividend income to the individual.

An Example. Consider the tax to be paid on a net business income (that is, after all expenses and deductions) of $100,000 in both a sole proprietorship and a corporation. In a sole proprietorship, the income tax would be imposed directly on the proprietor in his individual income tax return. Assuming that he has other income which exactly equals his nonbusiness deductions, so that the entire income is subject to tax, the sole proprietor would pay an income tax of around $45,000 on a joint return. Now assume that the business were a corporation so that the business income would be reported as the same $100,000 except a $30,000 salary paid to the owner. Two calculations are required to obtain the total tax burden. After the corporation pays a $30,000 salary to the owner; $70,000 is subject to tax on the corporate level; the corporate tax probably would be about $27,000. The $30,000 salary is also taxable on the individual income return of the owner-manager. If, as in the former case, his nonbusiness deductions are offset by other income so that his entire salary is subject to tax, the owner will pay about $7,900 in taxes on his salary on a joint return. The two taxes on the $100,000 of business profit thus total about $34,900; the current tax advantage of the corporate form is $45,000 less $34,900, or about $10,000.

In small, closely held corporations that do not pay dividends because of the great need for capital within the business, the owner-manager must pay a capital gains tax if he sells or liquidates the firm. However, if his ownership interest is passed on to his heirs, the estate may have to pay death taxes on the total value, but will pay no tax on the increase in the value of the business (capital gain) during the life of the owner. Thus, income will have been converted into capital without taxation at ordinary rates.

If a corporation meets certain Internal Revenue Service requirements, it may elect to have its income taxed directly to its shareholders, like a partnership under the Subchapter S option. Because of the complexities of the Internal Revenue Code and the opinions of the courts, the owner-manager should seek professional tax advice if he is considering a major change in the form of his business. Once the owner has set his long-range financial objectives, he must decide what particular form of business organization will best satisfy them. If he wants to build a strong firm with the eventual intention of "going public," then he should choose the corporate form of organization and establish financial and operating policies accordingly.

Other Decisions. Other important decisions that will influence the firm's financial and tax picture will need to be made on the following:

Establishing a fiscal year.
Values in using a Subchapter S Corporation.
Method of accounting, either cash or accrual.
Depreciation policies, including investment credits that may be available, the use of second-hand machinery and equipment.
Inventory valuing method—FIFO, LIFO.
Lease and purchase opportunities.
Buy-sell arrangements when there is more than one owner.
Liquidation and sale of business.
Acquisition of other firms.

The tax problem involved in each of these decisions must be carefully considered for its impact on the firm and on the owner-manager as an individual.

The owner-manager must also decide what his personal salary should be. If he wants to build the firm, he will draw a lower salary than if he wants merely to maintain the firm at a given operating level and draw a large salary. The firm's ability to borrow funds on its own statement will be related to its operating profits; and these will be reduced if the owner-manager withdraws large amounts for his own salary.

Management Decisions

The owner-manager of a firm should understand its basic accounting and operating policies so that he can make the kind of management moves regarding taxation that fit into his long-range program. Among the decisions affected by the provisions of the Internal Revenue Code are:

Purchase of equipment to take advantage of investment credit, leasing or outright purchase decisions.

Repair and maintenance of machinery and equipment, regarding expensing or capitalization of work performed.

Repair and maintenance of real estate, regarding expensing or capitalization of work performed.

Valuation of inventory for monthly and yearend financial statements.

Depreciation of new and used machinery and equipment.

Depreciation of real estate.

Sale or liquidation of assets above or below depreciated values.

Valuation of collectibility of accounts receivable in setting up bad debt reserves.

Determining the real value of research and development for capitalization or for expensing of the costs when incurred.

Valuation of tools, machinery and equipment built within the plant for purposes of capitalization or expensing of costs as incurred.

Sources of Tax Information and Assistance

The owner-manager is responsible for his firm's compliance with Federal, State, and local tax regulations. The burden of withholding, recording, reporting, and remitting taxes will fall on him or on the person he designates—such as his secretary, bookkeeper, or accountant. In addition to keeping the proper records, the owner-manager will need to use a tax calendar that will remind him when tax obligations fall due. This is particularly important in fast growing small firms.

Internal Tax Information Systems

Good accounting and control systems are vital in helping you determine the correct tax liability of your business. The Internal Revenue Service requires that a firm's statements on various tax forms be supported by permanent records. These must show clearly such information as: income, deductions, credits, inventories, sales or rentals subject to excise taxes, and names, addresses, and Social Security numbers of employees.

The owner-manager should consider having the firm's fiscal-year end during low inventory periods and slack seasons so as to avoid the extra burden of gathering tax information during busy periods. Knowing when the various reports are required and what they should include will allow him to balance his office's work load and avoid unnecessary overtime and undue work pressures. Frequently, it is helpful to hire part-time employees to work on the tax reports or to assume some of the routine tasks of the bookkeeper while he works on them.

External Sources of Tax Information and Advice

The owner-manager's need for outside tax information and assistance will vary with his own tax experience and that of his staff. Sources of tax information and assistance within the community may include:

Internal Revenue Service.
State and local tax agencies.
Libraries, public and private.
Trade associations.
Various U.S. Government agencies.
Banks.
Tax information services.

The value of these sources depends upon the owner-manager's willingness to seek and use the available information. Although some of these sources may not have up-to-the-minute information on the most recent tax court decisions, they can be of real value in obtaining tax opinions on various tax questions, current tax regulations, and suggestions on the development of the necessary tax records and systems.

The firm's basic source of tax assistance is usually the accountant. Complex tax questions may need the advice of one or more of the following sources:

Tax attorney.
Tax consulting firms.
Banker.
Internal Revenue Service.
State and local tax authorities.
Trade association tax specialist.
Supplier's legal department.

Frequently, an owner-manager will have a "fee fear" of using professionals; but he should always consider the long range economic effects of tax questions before refusing to seek outside advice. Because he sometimes faces tax questions that will affect his personal income all the way through to his estate, he should choose a tax adviser very carefully.

Summary

The businessman should recognize that tax laws are an important factor in his business planning. He must take them into consideration as he plans current and future courses of action. He should above all, be aware of the important difference between *tax evasion* (the failure to pay taxes due) and *tax avoidance* (an attempt to minimize the tax burden within the limits of established regulations). Taxation is an extremely technical, complex, and changing subject. It requires the continuous attention of a professional tax authority to keep up to date on Treasury decisions, court decisions, and new legislation at Federal, State, and local levels.

The owner-manager should carefully develop a long-range tax plan for himself and his firm. Many tax decisions that he must make in the operation of his business may have long-range affects on his estate. He will benefit by knowing clearly what his long-range plans are.

The owner-manager should realize the importance of tax information and advice to his management. He can develop his knowledge of tax matters by reading, by attending various tax workshops, and by working with other businessmen. In addition, he must organize and train his office staff in matters of tax collection, withholding, recording, reporting, and remittance. His bookkeeper or accountant, can be very helpful by maintaining a tax calendar and a plan of cash requirements so that the firm's tax reporting and tax payment obligations will be met on time.

Tax advisers can help the owner manager make long-range and day-to-day tax decisions. Generally, the first source of tax assistance will be the firm's outside accountant. Other specialists include tax attorneys, the Internal Revenue Service, tax consulting firms, and so forth.

Chapter 9

MANAGEMENT OF INSURANCE

BUSINESSMEN operate under constant risk, for there is no certainty of profit and no certainty of success. Goods purchased or produced must be sold; debts must be collected; natural and competitive hazards must be met and overcome. The owner-manager of a small firm must learn how to use the various available kinds of insurance to reduce the effects of these risks. Unexpected losses in a small firm can mean the difference between growth and failure. The owner-manager must broaden his personal knowledge of insurance management so that he can develop a balanced program for the ever-changing conditions in his firm.

Dealing With Business Risks

There are two major types of risks that the small business owner-manager faces: pure risk and speculative risk. Pure risk exists when a person is faced with a situation in which he has only the possibility of loss. Theft, bankruptcy of a customer, a fire, or the sickness or death of an owner or keyman are examples. Little can be done to stop pure risk, although management can take action to minimize it. Just by owning an automobile, a firm faces the risk of accident. Just by owning machinery, equipment, and buildings, a firm faces the possibility of accident, fire, and other hazards.

Speculative risk exists where there is the possibility of gain as well as loss. Investments in common stocks and real estate can yield either a profit or a loss. With speculative risks, the owner-manager can decide whether or not to subject his assets to loss. He can exercise a measure of control over risks; and for that reason, he usually cannot get an insurance policy to cover them. If it were otherwise, an owner-manager, no matter how poorly he ran his business, could insure himself against the risk of losing his capital and thus obtain a guarantee against failure.

It would be impossible for most any businessman to cover all of his potential risk. The amount of money he would have to set aside would leave him very little to run his business with. If he did suffer a loss that he could repair by using his reserve fund, what assurance would he have that another loss—the same kind or different—would not occur next week or next month? If it did, he would have no reserve fund, and little likelihood of staying in business at all.

The Role of Insurance

Insurance, then, plays a vital role in forestalling the damage that the unexpected can do. A well-conceived insurance program not only provides for losses, but sometimes also brings collateral values that are difficult to achieve through other means. For example, property, liability, theft, and business continuation insurance plans have corollary values in addition to their primary ones. And employee health and life insurance plans can be used—as added compensation—to reduce employee turnover and improve morale.

Lacking funds for total coverage, the owner-manager must develop a planned approach to risk management. He may be surprised at the many alternatives open to him for protection against risk.

The owner-manager must always be mindful of his program of risk management, and he must regularly remind his employees of the need to reduce the firm's exposure to risk. Periodically, he should evaluate his insurance program to keep it abreast of changes in the type and size of risks that the firm faces. He must always be alert to losses that could arise from carelessness. For example, failing to check for locked doors and closed windows, failing to keep oily materials in closed containers, and failing to maintain adequate supervision (leading to pilferage) are but a few of the things that may cause losses for the firm.

Various Types of Risks

In addition to pure and speculative, risks may also be classified as internal and external. For example, fire, theft, accidents, and bad debts may be considered internal; price changes, technological changes, labor unrest, legislative changes, competitors' activities, etc., are external risks, which, by and large, cannot be controlled. Risks may also be grouped according to whether they represent a possible loss of earning power or property (see figure 14).

For the small firm the most common risks are:

1. Business fraud and theft.
2. Fire.
3. Bad debts.
4. Legal liability.
5. Business interruptions.
6. Death or loss of key personnel.
7. Violent weather—flood, hurricane, tornado, etc.
8. Obsolete products and processes.

Of these, business fraud and theft, bad debts, and obsolete products and processes can be controlled by the owner-manager. Because of his closeness to employees and customers, the owner-manager of a small firm frequently fails to recognize the risks he faces from these sources. As a result, he fails to protect himself against losses from them.

Purchasing Coverage

In purchasing insurance, the boss should keep in mind the following:

1. Cover the largest loss exposure first, consistent with the cost of premium and funds available for protection. Be sure that on property coverage, valuations are adequate and liability coverage limits are high enough in relation to current court awards.

2. Use deductibles where applicable.

3. Review coverage periodically because of changes within the firm.

4. Review policy terms and provisions because of changes in the risk exposures on insurer's contracts.

5. Keep posted on the competitive activities of insurance companies.

6. Be aware of the firm's reduced loss experience; use it to get lower insurance premiums or as a basis for changing to another method of insurance.

7. Determine value of purchasing coverage in large blocks.

Figure 14—Types of Business Risk and Insurance Protection

Type of Risk	Form of Protection
Loss of earning power	Business interruption insurance Profits insurance Rent insurance Life insurance on key personnel
Loss of property (Destruction or damage)	Fire insurance Marine insurance Windstorm insurance Tornado insurance Explosion insurance Riot and insurrection insurance Automobile, fire and collision insurance Aircraft insurance Property depreciation insurance
Theft or infidelity	Auto theft insurance Burglary, theft insurance Forgery insurance Fidelity insurance
Failure of others	Credit insurance Surety bonding Title insurance
Loss of property (Legal liability)	Workmen's compensation insurance Employers' liability insurance Contractual liability Public liability insurance Advertiser's liability Automobile liability insurance Power plant insurance Elevator insurance Product liability insurance Sports liability insurance Physicians' insurance Aircraft insurance

A Program of Risk Management

Purchasing insurance gives a firm the opportunity to trade a large but uncertain loss for a small (but certain) loss (expenditure) called the premium. There are four methods of dealing with risk:

1. Commercial insurance.
2. Noninsurance (the firm assumes the risk).
3. Transfer of risk.
4. Self-insurance.

As a program of risk management is developed, all four methods may well be used. Application of a particular method, either for loss of property or loss of earning power, will de pend upon the owner-manager's judgement of his firm's needs at a particular time.

What Insurance Offers

For a fee, an insurance firm will assume responsibility for losses incurred from many types of risks. The insurance firm operates on the basis of the statistical chances that a specific type of loss will occur. Experience will determine whether or not an insurer will assume a given risk and what premium will be charged. The premium for a certain kind of coverage will depend upon the particular conditions in a situation. Against the cost of the premium for coverage of a given risk, the owner-manager must weigh his ability to reduce the probability of loss. Premiums for certain risks may be predicated on the insurance industry's experience with larger firms, while the owner-manager's close contact with his firm's operations may serve to keep his loss risk very low. Loss-prevention programs will seldom eliminate all losses, but they can often reduce them sufficiently to lower the cost of commercial insurance protection.

Noninsurance. Noninsurance, the firm's assumption of certain risks, should be based upon the firm's ability to control the potential loss or the fact that the loss, if incurred, would not seriously affect the business. Decisions to assume large risks simply because of the high cost of insurance can cause serious damage to the business. Noninsurance usually is confined to risks that are more or less predictable, preventable, or largely controllable. It is ideally suited to risks which are essentially "business risks"—those where the owner-manager has an opportunity to calculate his risk before making a given business decision. As a practical matter, when a firm is small, it must often assume many risks for which insurance protection is uneconomical. As the firm grows, such risks should be brought under a proper plan of protection at the appropriate time.

Risk Transfer. Transfer of risk to persons other than commercial insurers, a practice very common among small firms, is both practical and economical. For example, an owner-manager can transfer the risk or loss from automobile accidents by leasing his vehicles from a firm which will maintain all insurance. The lessor, insuring many automobiles, can get a significantly lower rate on coverage. Leases also can be used for buildings, equipment, and other assets. When a firm purchases services such as office cleanup or repair of machinery or equipment, it can transfer the risks to the firm supplying the service.

Retailers can reduce their cost of insuring inventories by adopting, when possible, a program of "hand to mouth" buying, which shifts the burden of risk to the wholesaler or manufacturer. In some cases, it may be possible to get the distributor or manufacturer to drop ship certain goods—thus further reducing the retailer's risk. Or it may be possible to get suppliers or customers to assume the risk, and insurance cost, for certain shipments.

Self-Insurance. Self-insurance differs from noninsurance. In noninsurance, a firm assumes a risk and does nothing about it; in self-insurance, it actually administers a program of risk management. A successful program would require:

1. A large number of similar jobs exposed to risk (enabling an accurate forecast of losses from year to year).
2. Sufficient financial strength to meet losses as they occur.
3. Giving one person the responsibility and authority to supervise a self-insurance program.

Economic opportunities for self-insurance in small firms will not be frequent. Usually, the number of employees doing any one job is not great enough; and the financail strength of many firms is too limited to set aside sufficient funds for the coverage needed. It would be definitely inadvisable for the owner-manager of an under-financed firm to try to save money by using self-insurance instead of paying the premiums for commercial insurance.

Because of the three requirements listed above, self-insurance is usually used only by large companies. The owner-manager of a small company will seldom have loss in one area frequently enough to make self-insurance practical.

Developing a Risk Management Program

The possibilities of loss prevail 24 hours a day, 7 days a week. Hoping they will disappear will not lessen them in any way, nor will the attitude "it can't happen here." Time and time again, owner-managers, experiencing unexpected and ruinous perils, wish they had been foresighted enough to extablish a program of risk management.

Such a program must consist of the following:

Recognizing major and minor risks.

Planning how to handle them.

Assigning specific authority and responsibility to specific key employees.

Keeping all employees aware of the program.

Reviewing the risk management program periodically.

Adapting the program to changing conditions.

The internal program must be planned, organized, directed, coordinated, and controlled by the owner-manager or one of his professional insurance advisers. Each person involved in the program must be educated through reading and training sessions so that he will understand the elements involved in insurance and risk management. Incentives should be provided for members of the firm to make significant contributions to the reduction of losses.

Activities that would contribute to loss prevention would include:

Establishing and maintaining a safety program.

Setting up and enforcing safe work rules in the shop and office.

Measuring the firm's success in avoiding specific risks.

Keeping employees posted on their performance.

Bonding employees who handle cash or materials.

Keeping employees "loss conscious."

Maintaining clean and uncluttered offices and shop.

Developing and maintaining proper accounting records and operating control reports.

Keeping accurate asset-value records—including data on repairs and improvements.

Searching for new and more effective ways to reduce risks in all phases of the operation.

Trying to reduce employee turnover to a minimum—so as to reduce workmen's compensation and other costs associated with labor turnover.

Developing an atmosphere in which all accidents, no matter how minor, are reported to management.

These suggestions are a small sample of the actions the owner-manager can take to reduce risks in his firm.

Willingness to spend time on improving risk management and to use professionals in setting up an insurance program can pay cash dividends over the long run. Most insurance companies are ready and able to furnish technical assistance on the establishment of a risk management program. It takes considerable time to establish and put in action such a program. But once the necessary discipline is being maintained and the elements of the program periodically reviewed, the firm should benefit by experiencing fewer losses and by paying lower insurance premiums.

Working With Professional Insurance Agents or Brokers

In working with professional insurance agents or brokers, an owner-manager should know what they can do for him. One way to gain knowledge is by reading about the types of agents.

Types of Agents

The various types of insurance are handled by either the independent agent (or broker) or the direct writer. The independent agent represents the insurer, and the broker is the legal representative of the party to be insured. When a firm employs a broker to secure insurance, it is legally bound by the broker's acts. Technically, the broker cannot "bind" coverage automatically as can the agent. Many agents are also brokers; most brokers are also agents.

The independent agent may deal directly with the insurer, with a general agent, or with a branch office that has been authorized to represent the insurer. The insurer maintains no direct control over the business of the agent other than to decide what business it will accept or reject. The agent is independent, as is the broker. The agent may and usually does represent several insurers. His clients belong to him, and the insurer cannot appoint another agent to take over his accounts. Usually, the local agent grants credit to the insurance buyer. Frequently, he has considerable authority to issue policies, change the terms of contracts, and "bind" insurance after an oral agreement between himself and the client.

Direct writers are insurers that sell directly to the customer through the mails or through salaried or commissioned salesmen. Salesmen are employees of the insurer and not independent businessmen. Any policy they write does not belong to them, but to the insurer—who, at will, may turn it over to another employee.

Types of Insurance Companies

The four major types of insurers in the United States are:

Stock companies.
Mutual companies.
Reciprocals.
Lloyd's groups.

Stock companies, which are chartered in the various States, are profitmaking corporations. Mutual companies are owned by policyholders and are chartered as nonprofit institutions under the laws of the various States. Reciprocals, sometimes called interinsurance exchanges, are associations of individuals (typically specialists in a particular type of risk) who exchange contracts of insurance and more or less insure one another's risks. Lloyd's groups are composed of individual underwriters. In general, mutual companies and reciprocals are cooperatively organized insurers and offer insurance at cost, while stock companies and Lloyd's groups are profitmaking ventures. In practice, the costs of the cooperatively owned insurer may be no lower than those of the profitmaking insurer.

Insurance companies, like banks, are subject to stringent government regulations whose purpose is to protect the customer. Insurance agents and brokers must be licensed. Insurance companies must be incorporated; their funds, rates, policies, and accounting methods are checked regularly.

Working With Professionals

Recognizing the complexity of insurance and risk management, the owner manager should seek the professional assistance of insurance counselors, brokers, agents, suppliers, and/or trade association insurance specialists. Working with professionals will keep him up-to-date on changes in insurance coverage practices. And he can be more certain that he is keeping the proper insurance records up-to-date and that he has adequate coverage to take care of any sudden loss. (Figure 15 gives major sources of information and assistance on various aspects of insurance.)

Summary

The owner-manager of a small business must give serious consideration to insurance and risk management; a successful program requires organization and planning; it does not come to pass through accident.

Figure 15—Sources of Information and Assistance on Insurance

Assistance Needed	Source
Explanation of policy terminology Comparison of cost of different types of policies Survey of firm's exposures to loss	Local agents, brokers, independent insurance counselors
Help in firm's loss-prevention program	Local agents, representatives of insurers, engineers
Help in collection on losses for which insurer denies liability	State insurance commissioner, local agents, attorneys
Information about insurer— Finances Type of coverage offered Flexibility in coverage offered Cost of coverage	State insurance commissioners, bank officers, brokers, local agents, representatives of insurers

The owner-manager must recognize the various ways in which his firm can suffer losses, and he must decide how he will use insurance and risk management to forestall them. He must understand the various available ways of dealing with risks: commercial insurance, noninsurance, risk transfer, and self-insurance. And he should recognize the value of training his employees to be "loss conscious."

The owner-manager will find it invaluable to develop a close working relationship with professional insurance counselors, brokers, and agents. He should understand the roles of the independent agent, the broker, and the direct writer. And he should know, in general, how the major types of insurers differ: stock companies, mutual companies, reciprocals and Lloyd's groups.

Chapter 10

LEGAL ASPECTS OF BUSINESS OPERATION

MOST decisions made by the small businessman have their legal aspects. Legal questions appear when there are any of the following problems or conditions: form of organization (sole proprietorship, partnership, or corporation), taxes, leases, real estate, delinquent accounts, insurance contracts, estates and wills, purchase agreements, sales contracts, franchises, general contracts and agreements, and formal litigation. Daily transactions with customers, suppliers, employees, and the general public expose any firm to many legal risks. Members of a firm must be aware of local, State and Federal laws and regulations that apply to the firm's activities.

The discussion here will be on the broad aspects of law and business; it will not deal with the details of law, but will touch on the various ways the owner-manager can seek advice on his legal problems.

The Legal Aspects of Business

Hardly a business decision is made that does not have legal aspects. Purchasing, sales arrangements, real estate leases, license arrangements, labor contracts, long-term bank financing—all involve decisions having legal import. The owner-manager should be aware of the legal problems related to his company's size, trade, and geographical location. He must bear in mind that ignorance of the law is not accepted as an excuse and that even licensed attorneys are not always sure of certain provisions of the law and their interpretation by the courts.

Laws in the United States are grouped under two broard classifications: criminal law and civil law. Criminal law deals with acts (crimes) considered injurious to society. For such acts society imposes a penalty such as imprisonment or a fine. Criminal laws are enforced through society's authorized courts and law enforcement officers. Civil law is concerned with protecting the individual, especially his rights and private property. Civil law provides that damages for injury sustained may be secured by the person concerned through bringing suit against the offender.

Acts passed by a Federal or State lawmaking body and constitutional provisions included in the original Federal and State constitutions and their amendments are called statutes. Many statutes that have been enacted charge a special board, commission, or agency to administer the law. For example, the Clayton Act is administered by the Federal Trade Commission; the National Labor Relations Act is administered by the National Labor Relations Board. The common law leading to justice and fair treatment may govern in situations not covered by a specific legal enactment.

Principal Legal Problems

The owner manager should understand the principles of law (whether Federal, State, or local) dealing with licenses, taxes, contracts, bills of sale, mortgages, etc., so that he can carry on his activities without breaking the law, and so that he will not sacrifice the rights and benefits to which he is legally entitled. He should be particularly aware of legal implications of the following:

Type of business organization.
Taxes.
Real estate transactions.
Collection of delinquent accounts.
Insurance policies.
Contracts and agreements.
Formal litigation.
Estates and wills.

For example, real estate transactions are generally long-run business commitments which will have an important effect on the success or failure of the firm. Whether they deal with purchase or sale or with leasing (as a tenant *or* a landlord), such transactions are subject to many unknowns. The neces-

Figure 16—Sources of Legal Problems

Acquisitions
Advertising—copy packaging
Agents and brokers
Antitrust matters
Arbitration—role in disputes
Bankruptcy
Board of directors
Brand names
Buying and selling—terms and conditions
Checks—forgeries, frauds
Contracts and agreements
Competitors stealing employees
Corporate form
Employer and employee responsibilities
Employment agreements
Franchises
Government—Federal, State, and local
Insurance contracts
Interstate transportation
Inventions
Labeling
Licenses
Mergers
Misrepresentation
Multiple corporations
Negligence
Negotiable instruments
Order acknowledgment and confirmation
Patents
Permits
Price discrimination
Profit sharing
Product liability
Records, legal
Retirement pensions
Slander and libel
Stock options
Stock voting rights
Stockholders
Taxes
Tie-in sales
Trade secrets
Trademarks
Unfair competition
Verbal agreements
Wills
Workmen's compensation
Zoning

sary legal documents must be prepared in such a way as to limit the owner-manager's exposure to liability. This takes great care, the time of the principals, and the services of a skilled attorney. Reducing such exposure to liability is not a "do-it-yourself" job. (Figure 16 lists areas of interest that involve legal consideration.)

To avoid litigation—particularly unwarranted suits—the owner-manager should know exactly the extent and limit of his responsibilities to suppliers, customers, employees, etc. The owner-manager must keep an eye on the customs of trades other than his own. For example, when a retail merchant uses an advertising agency, he encounters practices special to the advertising business. When a manufacturer buys a special component from a vendor and pays for special tooling, the vendor keeps possession of the tooling. Terms of payment vary by trades. For example, normal trade practice among grocery suppliers is to require payment in 7 days; but soft goods manufacturers normally have much longer terms, such as 2 percent 10, net 30.

Solving Legal Problems

The owner-manager's awareness of the laws and regulations within which his firm operates will help him to know when he is making a decision that might later involve some formal litigation.

Recognizing Legal Problems

There will be little doubt in certain business situations that legal aspects are involved. It may be the nature of the transaction, such as a special contract or bill of sale, or perhaps a special type of negotiable instrument. It may be a transaction requiring professional help—such as a real estate deal, bank loan, or a licensing transaction. Or it may be a situation that involves large sums of money, one on which the owner-manager wants to seek legal assistance.

In any case, the owner-manager must determine whether to handle the problem himself or seek outside advice. As part of his decision, he will naturally consider the risk involved in the transaction. If it is minor, he may decide to take a chance. He should, however, recognize all the factors before he makes a decision. One of the best ways he can prepare himself to make these decisions is to take a course in business law. Almost all colleges and business schools offer such courses.

Keeping aware of business law is at best a difficult job. The owner-manager has little time to read about a field that is constantly changing because of court decisions and statutory changes. A good rule of thumb is for the owner-manager to watch his trade journal for articles on major legal changes that effect his industry and check with his lawyer.

The owner-manager must try to avoid legal entanglements from any source because they are not only a strain on the firm's relations with customers and suppliers, but are also a drain on the owner-manager's time and on the firm's funds.

Reducing Legal Problems

Every owner-manager need not be a lawyer, but he should be able to recognize potential legal problems that might develop from certain business situations and then be prepared to take the necessary steps to avoid or minimize his risk.

Systems and procedures can help reduce legal problems involving customers, suppliers, employees, and others. For example, the retailer who fails to have customers sign for goods they take to "try out" is in a vulnerable legal position if the customers damage the goods or fail to return them. To have proof of delivery, the retailer should insist on a signature for such goods. Then should any problems develop, he will be protected.

The boss must recognize the advantage of *avoiding* litigation whenever possible. This will not only save him time, but will also avoid jeopardizing the firm's relationship with the many people with whom it does business.

A properly drawn agreement or contract can help avert litigation. If a matter is too small for a formal agreement, an exchange of letters may be useful. It is impractical to legalize every business transaction, but it is vital for the owner-manager to be aware of his exposure and to put important agreements in writing.

Sources of Legal Assistance

With reasonable interest and effort, the small business owner-manager can gain an understanding of the more important statutes and regulations that affect his firm. However, when complex problems develop, he will want to call upon competent legal counsel or upon the appropriate nonlegal adviser.

The owner-manager's selection of legal counsel involves some consideration. Should he retain a large law firm having tax, labor, credit, patent, and bankruptcy specialists? Should he seek the services of a small firm of generalists? Or should he employ a lawyer who practices as an individual? His decision will be based mainly on (1) the size and legal needs of his business, (2) his evaluation of a particular lawyer's experience and its relation to his firm's needs, and (3) a sensible fee relationship. Many legal firms and individual lawyers work with small firms for very reasonable fees because they expect that as the firm grows so will their fees.

There are significant advantages to a firm in having a continuing relationship with an attorney. As a lawyer gets to know more about a firm, its employees, customers, suppliers, and previous contracts and agreements, he can give advice quickly and more effectively. Also, for a firm, the cost of legal advice is apt to be reduced if there is a continuing relationship with counsel. Moreover, when the owner-manager has an annual review of operations with his attorney, he may become able to handle repetitive problems without having to go to his lawyer constantly for advice.

A Close Working Relationship

The advantage of establishing a close working relationship becomes clear in the event of a suit against the firm, say for breach of contract. To suggest an effective course of action to the owner-manager, the attorney must be acquainted with all the elements of the business and trade as they relate to the suit and the contract. If the attorney has been associated with the firm long enough, he will be aware of the pertinent factors in the suit and will be able to reach an opinion more quickly. The attorney with a close relationship to a business can also be a sounding board for the owner-manager as he faces business decisions; certain problems can't be discussed with keymen. Many owner-managers use their attorney to negotiate important transactions such as purchasing real estate, leasing space, arranging a bank loan, or securing proper insurance coverage. The owner-manager can often make effective use of this technique of third party negotiation.

The use of other nonlegal advisers is common. Frequently, the owner-manager will develop a close relationship with his accountant, whose knowledge of the financial affairs of the business makes him a valuable source of tax advice. Of course, many accountants are not qualified to give general business advice; both accountant and businessman must make a judgment on this.

Other nonlegal advisers would probably include: the banker, insurance counselor, real estate broker, management consultant, suppliers, customers, and other business acquaintances. Each might be a source of valuable information in addition to acting as a sounding board for problems relating to their particular area of business. Once again, the more these advisers know of the firm's performance and interests, the more promptly they can give counsel applicable to the conditions at hand.

Summary

The owner-manager must be aware of the major and minor legal problems that exist in his business. He must also recognize the trade customs peculiar to his industry and their legal complications. He must be able to recognize the risks he is exposed to in dealing with customers, suppliers, employees, and the public at large. And he must be aware of the many local, State, and Federal laws and regulations under which his firm operates.

Daily involvement in sales, operations, finance, and overall management leaves the owner-manager with little time to assume new responsibilities. But he must understand the importance of the legal aspects of his business. He should know the various legal points involved in his day-to-day and long-run decisions. He must decide whether he will improve his own understanding of law or whether he will delegate some of the responsibility to his attorney or other nonlegal advisers.

The owner-manager should try to be sure that he or his key subordinates can cope with legal questions as they develop. Someone must decide whether a particular situation involves major or minor legal matters. Someone must be able to determine the degree of exposure the firm faces when legal problems arise. If this skill is lacking in management, serious consequences could later develop.

The owner-manager can take additional steps to reduce legal problems for his firm. He should install efficient systems and procedures; he should manage his firm with discipline; he should always make careful decisions when he faces a major legal risk, and when he is going to sign a contract or make a written commitment.

Many sources of legal assistance are available to the owner-manager of the small firm. He can work with an attorney from a large law firm that has on its staff tax, labor, credit, patent, and other specialists; he can work with a lawyer from a small firm of generalists; or he can work with a lawyer who practices as an individual. Whichever he chooses, it is important to establish a close continuing relationship with the attorney.

The owner-manager gets good value from a close legal relationship because his lawyer will be aware of many aspects of his business and will be able to give him quicker and more carefully reasoned opinions. Close knowledge of trade customs, a firm's customers, suppliers, and employees, and its contractual relationships cannot but help to improve the lawyer's services.

In many problems of legal nature, the service of nonlegal advisers may be very helpful. These outside advisers may include accountants, bankers, insurance advisers, advertising or trade association staff members, real estate agents, management consultants, and business friends. Whether he uses legal or nonlegal advisers, the owner-manager should take advantage of the many sources of specialized skills that exist in his community. Although it may take time to establish an effective advisory group, the rewards are many and measurable.